Reflections on Fieldwork in Morocco

Paul Rabinow

Reflections on Fieldwork in Morocco

With a Foreword by Robert N. Bellah

Tu le connais, lecteur, ce monstre délicat,
—hypocrite lecteur—mon semblable, mon frère
BAUDELAIRE

University of California Press
Berkeley · Los Angeles · London

1 2 3 4 5 6 7 8 9

This book is dedicated to my Moroccan companions, whose names have been changed here to protect their anonymity.

The following people have been particularly generous and helpful: Robert Bellah, Jean-Paul Dumont, Kevin Dwyer, Clifford Geertz, Eugene Gendlin, Sherry Ortner, Robert Paul, Gwen Wright. Most of all I wish to thank Paul Hyman, for his stunning and perceptive pictures, his acute and unique insights, and his friendship.

Contents

Foreword

Paul Rabinow, in a suggestive phrase borrowed from Paul Ricoeur, sums up the problem of interpretation and the problem of this book: "the comprehension of the self by the detour of the comprehension of the other." Most of the book, quite rightly given its aim, is concerned with the enormous difficulties and complexities involved in the comprehension of the other. Only allusively do we see that the project of the comprehension of the other has been motivated by a profound perplexity about the comprehension of the self. Here I speak, as does the author, not of the personal, psychological self, but of the cultural self. Much of the best work in anthropology (as in sociology and psychology) has been motivated by a deepening sense of that perplexity. Perhaps the most poignant thing about this book is that by the penultimate chapter it becomes clear that the author (speaking for the cultural, not the personal self) does not have a "my culture" to complement the indubitably "your culture" of even the most modernized Moroccan villager. In consolation for that desolating realization we are offered just a glimpse of the idea that having lost a traditional "my culture," the modern Western intellectual has available the totality of cultures for personal appropriation. That, of course, is what the

"detour" is all about. But the author is too aware of
the difficulties of understanding, much less of appropriation, and of the violent possibilities inherent
in the very idea of appropriation for him to offer us
any ready reassurance.

The book is set chronologically between the realization by the author, just before departing for the
field, that the noble effort to revive "the great tradition" at the University of Chicago had failed and the
realization just after his return that the radical ideol-
ogy with which so many modern intellectuals attempt to clothe their cultural nakedness has also
failed. Neither a forced resurrection of "my culture"
(Western civilization) nor an apocalyptic and revolutionary substitute for it have worked. The detour
seems more necessary than ever, but none of us
knows how far it will take us before we find the way.
In the penultimate chapter we get a glimpse of
another detour, Vietnam, seductively waiting to be
explored.

And yet the shadows that are never too far in the
background of this book do not make it a depressing
one. What gives hope is not any false consolation
offered by the author but the sheer exhilarating fact
that he could write it at all, so simply and unpreten-
tiously, when to write such a book seems hardly possible for a generation only a little older. It is as if the
proclamations of my teachers and contemporaries—
that culture is a human thing, that it is human beings
that create it, interpret it, and change it—had suddenly become alive. No longer sentences in a book,
they have been embodied and made real to become
new kinds of sentences in a new kind of book. We all

know that field data (or any other kind of data in the human studies for that matter) are not *Dinge an sich* but are constructs of the process by which we acquire them. But here we see beautifully illuminated that process at work.

I particularly admire the way in which the author can reveal just so much as we need to know of his personal feelings and judgments without ever obtruding parts of himself that are not relevant to the process of cultural understanding. Rabinow not only shows a degree of being at ease with himself that many of us lack, he also makes the important point that knowing in the human studies is always emotional and moral as well as intellectual. The emotional honesty that anyone who has ever worked in the field at once recognizes should alone recommend the book to the anxious anthropological novice. Even more important is the unselfconsciousness about the moral dimension that I take to be the most valuable contribution of the book. Fieldwork, like any investigation in the human studies, involves constant valuation and revaluation. Many of us, frightened by Weber's contempt for those who use the lecture platform for political or religious prophecy, have forgotten that value neutrality had for Weber a very specific and a very confined meaning, namely the obligation not to let our value predilections dictate the results of our research, and that it was itself a moral norm, a tenet in the ethics of scholarship. What is dangerous is not the presence of value judgments—they can be found in almost every line that Weber wrote—but only those judgments that remain beyond the reach of critical reflection and are not subject to revision in the light of experience. In this book we see not only the inevitable presence of moral judgment but the process whereby that judgment is itself educated and deepened. The Moroccans with whom Rabinow worked were not only fellow artificers of the cultural product that the fieldwork produced, they were also in part his teachers in what it is to be human, as he was, to an extent, theirs.

There is, finally, one other barrier that this modest book helps to tear down—the barrier between scholarship and poetry. If the author has reminded us quite rightly that a fact is, etymologically, something that is "made," we may be forgiven for pointing out that the Greek word *poiēsis* means "making" and that the poet is a "maker." But the materials of the poet are not so much facts as symbols and narratives, or rather facts that are themselves symbols and narratives. In the human studies to deny any noetic value to symbols and narratives is to reduce human things to physical things, action to motion. Rabinow does not make that mistake. The symbols, those outbreaking or inbreaking moments that concentrate the meaning of the tale, and the narrative structure itself, which follows one of the oldest of all mythic scenarios, the journey of the hero on a dangerous mission and his successful return, provide much of what is cognitively illuminating in the book. The departure from the traditional structure is as instructive as the recapitulation of the archetype. In legend the hero returns home and lives happily ever after. In this book, as we have seen, the hero returns to an even deeper doubt about the very meaning and existence of home than he had before he set out. Perhaps that tells us that the journeys we must now take must go farther and deeper than any that have gone before. In any case we remain in the author's debt for showing us so much with such simplicity and such grace.

Robert N. Bellah

Introduction

I left Chicago two days after the assassination of Robert Kennedy. My apartment in Chicago was practically bare. I had finished packing and had sold most of my furniture, leaving only the bed and a coffeepot. I had been mildly anxious about leaving, but the news of the murder had buried those feelings under a wave of revulsion and disgust. I left America with a sense of giddy release. I was sick of being a student, tired of the city, and felt politically impotent. I was going to Morocco to become an anthropologist.

I arrived in Paris in June of 1968, several days after police had cleared the last students from the faculty of medicine. In the wake of the uprising I found the streets nearly empty, and ripped-up walls covered with political graffiti. I attended several meetings in the courtyard of the Sorbonne, but it was too late, the revolutionary momentum had crested. Leaflets urged people not to leave Paris for their vacations. The capital was empty, broken, worn. I met a girl— part Indian, she said—who was running away from her home in Arizona. As we wandered by the Seine, the war-like atmosphere and uncertain future made me feel like a character in one of Sartre's novels, very existential. Two days later I had my hair cut, took the bus to Orly, and left for Morocco.

In the early 1960s the great Hutchins experiment in general education was in its last stages at the University of Chicago. Knowing that liberal education in its "classic" sense was dying out moved me deeply. The college had offered me the profound and liberating experience of discovering what thinking is really about, but it had also left me with a sense of crisis about the older sciences and disciplines. For most of us, it was slowly becoming clear that American society was beset with profound structural problems, and that the illumination and coherence necessary to overcome them would not be found in the academy or in existing political institutions. This left many of us searching and confused, but still relatively passive. The troubles ran deep, but Chicago was serene on the surface.

Perhaps the two books which expressed the ethos of that time most fully for me were Thomas Kuhn's *The Structure of Scientific Revolutions* (1962) and Claude Lévi-Strauss' *Tristes Tropiques* (1955). Kuhn had clearly isolated a set of concerns which extended beyond physics and chemistry. His term "paradigm exhaustion" symbolized the failure of conventional thinking to explain the common theme in our dissatisfactions with the academic curriculum, politics, and personal experience. Somehow, the received truths offered to us were not sufficient to organize our perceptions and experiences; something new must lie ahead.

My attraction to Lévi-Strauss's concept of *dépaysement* separated me from many of my friends, who were more enticed by the emerging varieties of social and political praxis. The Frenchman's paradoxical call for a distancing that would allow one to return more profoundly home was compelling, if obscure. I was weary of the West, without knowing why, and was seduced by the simplistic view that Western culture was only one among many, and not the most "interesting" one at that.

This undergraduate ennui plus my fervent intellectual bent had drawn me to anthropology. It seemed to be the only academic discipline where, by definition, one had to get out of the library and away from other academics. Its scope was truly preposterous, literally anything from lemur feet to shadow plays; as one professor put it, it was "the dilettante's discipline."

In the graduate anthropology department at the University of Chicago, the world was divided into two categories of people: those who had done fieldwork, and those who had not; the latter were not "really" anthropologists, regardless of what they knew about anthropological topics. Professor Mircea Eliade, for example, was a man of great erudition in the field of comparative religion, and was respected for his encyclopedic learning, but it was repeatedly stressed that he was not an anthropologist: his intuition had not been altered by the alchemy of fieldwork.

I was told that my papers did not really count because once I had done fieldwork they would be radically different. Knowing smiles greeted the acerbic remarks which graduate students made about the lack of theory in certain of the classics we studied; never mind, we were told, the authors were great fieldworkers. At the time, this intrigued me. The promise of initiation into the clan secrets was seductive. I fully accepted the dogma.

Yet I knew of no book which made a serious intellectual effort to define this essential rite of passage, this metaphysical marker which separated anthropologists from the rest. Undoubtedly the one great exception to this intriguing rule was Lévi-Strauss' masterpiece, *Tristes Tropiques.* Still, as everyone knew, Lévi-Strauss was not a good fieldworker. The book was treated by anthropologists either as a fine piece of French literature or, snidely and true to form, as an overcompensation for the author's shortcomings in the bush.

I have asked leading anthropologists who espouse this "before and after" view of fieldwork why they have not written on the subject themselves, since it seems to be such an important one for the field. The response I received was culturally standardized: "Yes, I suppose, I thought about it when I was young. I kept diaries, perhaps someday, but you know there are really other things which are more important."

This book is an account of my experiences in Morocco; it is also an essay about anthropology. I have tried to break through the double-bind which has defined anthropology in the past. As graduate students we are told that "anthropology equals experience"; you are not an anthropologist until you have the experience of doing it. But when one returns from the field, the opposite immediately applies: anthropology is not the experiences which made you an initiate, but only the objective data you have brought back.

One can let off steam by writing memoirs or anecdotal accounts of sufferings, but under no circumstances is there any direct relation between field activity and the theories which lie at the core of the discipline. In recent years there has been a minor flurry of books dealing with the question of participant observation. These books have varied a great deal in keenness of perception and grace of style, but they all cling to the key assumption that the field experience itself is basically separable from the mainstream of theory in anthropology—that the enterprise of inquiry is essentially discontinuous from its results.

At the risk of violating the clan taboos, I argue that all cultural activity is experiential, that fieldwork is a distinctive type of cultural activity, and that it is this activity which defines the discipline. But what should therefore be the very strength of anthropology—its experiential, reflective, and critical activity—has been eliminated as a valid area of inquiry by an attachment to a positivistic view of science, which I find radically inappropriate in a field which claims to study humanity.

The problem of the book is a hermeneutical one, and the method I employ is a modified phenomenological one. I have striven to keep the use of technical terms and jargon to an absolute minimum, but it seems only fair to give some signposts for the path I have attempted to travel. Thus, following Paul Ricoeur, I define the problem of hermeneutics (which is simply Greek for "interpretation") as "the comprehension of self by the detour of the comprehension of the other."* It is vital to stress that this is not psychology of any sort, despite the definite

---

*Paul Ricouer, "Existence et hermeneutique," p. 20, in *Le Conflit des Interpretations* (Editions Du Seuil, Paris, 1969).

psychological overtones in certain passages. The self being discussed is perfectly public, it is neither the purely cerebral cogito of the Cartesians, nor the deep psychological self of the Freudians. Rather it is the culturally mediated and historically situated self which finds itself in a continuously changing world of meaning.

For that reason I employ a phenomenological method. Ricoeur again offers us a clear definition. Phenomenology for him is a description of "a movement in which each cultural figure finds its meaning not in what precedes it but in what follows: consciousness is drawn out of itself and ahead of itself in a process in which each step is abolished and retained in the following one."* In simpler language, this means that what you will read in this book is meant to be a whole, in which the meaning of each chapter depends on what comes after it. What the book and these experiences are about is themselves.

The book is a reconstruction of a set of encounters that occurred while doing fieldwork. At that time, of course, things were anything but neat and coherent. At this time, I have made them seem that way so as to salvage some meaning from that period for myself and for others. This book is a studied condensation of a swirl of people, places, and feelings. It could have been half as long, or twice as long, or ten times as long. Some informants with whom I worked are not mentioned, some are collapsed into the figures presented here, and others are left out altogether. Anyone who had such a set of progressively coherent

Ibid., p. 25.

encounters while in the field, and was fully conscious of it at the time, would not have the kind of experience which I have reconstructed here. As Hegel says, "the owl of Minerva flies at Dusk."

What follows is an account, reconstructed five years later and again two years after that, of my fieldwork experience in Morocco during 1968 and 1969. I worked in Morocco under the guidance of my advisor, Clifford Geertz, who, along with his wife Hildred and two other young anthropologists, was studying a walled oasis market town, Sefrou. My task was to work in the tribal areas surrounding Sefrou in the Middle Atlas Mountains of Morocco.*

*For a complementary and more traditionally anthropological treatment of the data covered here, see my *Symbolic Domination: Cultural Form and Historical Change in Morocco* (University of Chicago Press, Chicago, 1975).

1. Remnants of a Dying Colonialism

The Sais plain which stretches over lightly rolling countryside between the cities of Fez and Sefrou (both founded in the ninth century A.D.) is one of the most fertile areas in Morocco. Its verdure totally belies any romantic imagery of desert tents or Moorish landscapes. Leaving the magnificent walled city of Fez, the landscape is more reminiscent of France. The Sais was one off the regions in which French colonial implantation had been most active, bringing mechanization, irrigation, and profit.

The regularly drawn fields, the rich dark soil, the elevated irrigation canals that snake along for miles, the grid-like patterns of orchards, and the occasional farmhouse exemplify perfectly what Jacques Berque has chosen as a symbol of the French colonial experience in North Africa: the land without people surrounded by the people without land.* The tile roofs of the scattered farmhouses stand in strong contrast to the clusters of farmworkers' mud and brick dwellings, which become more frequent as one moves along the Sais plane towards Sefrou. The farmhouses are still clearly set off by fences and the workers' quarters by cactus hedges, but the owners of the farms are no longer French. Much of this area

---

*See Jacques Berque, *Le Maghreb Entre Deux Guerres* (Editions Du Seuil, Paris, 1962).

had been nationalized and is run by the Moroccan government. The rest is owned by the affluent merchants of Fez.

Even after passing through this fertile countryside, one is struck by the lushness of the city of Sefrou as it appears on the horizon. It is hidden from view as one approaches from Fez. The hills are now somewhat more substantial and the vistas less sweeping and regular. Sefrou, with a population of some twenty-five thousand, is literally an oasis town. The richness of the irrigated Sais hides this fact at first; but behind Sefrou lie the Middle Atlas Mountains, which are now dry and largely deforested. A series of rocky, sparsely populated hills and plateaus lie to the south of Sefrou and lead to the mountains proper. Sefrou itself is located within a narrow piedmont which circles the lowest edge of the mountains and which is marked by a series of large springs which water sizable gardens, orchards, and olive groves. The Moroccans call such an ecological niche the *dir*—literally, the "breast." This niche follows a series of geological faults along the edge of the mountains. As one follows the line of the *dir*, one also follows a line of well-watered, climatically favored, and prosperous towns. Sefrou is such a town.

Because of its location Sefrou has served as a marketing and commercial center for the tribes in the surrounding region. In addition to the farmers who work the gardens of the oasis, and the merchants, it has traditionally had a large and active population of artisans. Sefrou has also had, as far back as the ninth century, a dynamic Jewish community which has often served as a link between the urban community and the rural Berber tribal groups. These Moroccan Jews activated an exchange of mountain products (wool, mutton, rugs) with imported and manufactured goods (textiles, tea, sugar).

French colonization of the farmlands around Sefrou—which began in the late 1920s and increased steadily until the 1950s—and the establishment of French governmental, commercial, and educational institutions in the town had a substantial impact on Sefrou's growth and direction. Following the colonial policy of Lyautey, they built new quarters, a Ville Nouvelle, alongside the older walled medina of Sefrou. They never colonized Morocco to the extent that they did Algeria, however. The French population of Sefrou in 1960, for example, was less than 1 percent, and this included the new wave of schoolteachers.

I was driven to the Hôtel de l'Oliveraie, perhaps one hundred yards outside the crenelated walls of Sefrou's medina. Old and drab, its paint cracking, L'Oliveraie was clearly a decaying edifice, yet it had its charm. One entered through a double jalousie doorway into a rectangular room divided approximately in half by a shabby screen. To the left were some ten neatly set tables (I never saw more than two in use) and to the right were a long wooden bar, several bare tables with old restaurant chairs, and a rickety pinball machine in the corner. All the windows had shutters, most half open, and the pall or quiet of the late afternoon hung over a besotted Moroccan cab driver, the only customer, at the moment of my arrival.

Emerging from behind the bar with a swift bow, neatly groomed but casually dressed, was Maurice

Richard, the owner of the hotel, the *patron*. Yes, he did have a room; in fact he had ten, would I follow him? Which shall it be, he mused, and a gentle charade began, although its hollowness and pathos were apparent from the start. Richard later showed me to one of the ten tables, holding the chair for me and graciously informing me that there was only one menu.

The next morning, my fourth in Morocco, I had coffee and bread in the courtyard of l'Oliveraie. It must have been lovely in earlier years. There was an enclosed garden with a grillwork from which vines once grew, there were metal tables which once shined, and there was Ahmed, the waiter, impeccably groomed, who might have served (or so I imagined) tables of French families preparing for the tasks of the day ahead. I was alone. It was already getting hot. Ahmed brought me the brown earthenware coffee pot with a polite, pseudo-French bow, refused my overtures, and moving swiftly, left.

How ethnographic. In Morocco only several days and already I was set up in a hotel, an obvious remnant of colonialism, was having my coffee in a garden, and had little to do but start "my" fieldwork. Actually, it was not exactly clear to me what that meant, except that I supposed I would wander around Sefrou a bit. After all, now that I was in the field, everything was fieldwork.

Whistling, moving his portly frame with speed and grace, Richard appeared from behind his jalousie doors, wished me "bon appetit," and handed me a tourist card to fill out. He was somewhat surprised that I was American. He was sure, he

Richard at ease in the Oliveraie,
the last French bar in Sefrou.

said, that I was an Eastern European (which I suppose I am, ethnically at least), and then he launched
into a hearty but cautious set of pleasantries.

The second day in Sefrou he told me his life story.
He was from an upper-middle-class Parisian family.
He had left home in 1950 to seek adventure, ending
up in Morocco, where he had followed a series of
professions ranging from mechanic to hotelkeeper.
The lack of the usual French reserve and hostility was
startlingly indicative, I mused, either of a transforma-
tion of French culture once it left France or an intense
loneliness on Richard's part. Here it was the loneliness which prevailed. It quickly emerged that he was
a Parisian *manqué*. The expectations his family of col-
onels and doctors had placed on him was too heavy
to bear, and so he had left them to wander through
an existence of assorted lower-middle-class trades.

He was also a failure historically; he had arrived in
Morocco a generation too late. The first wave of
French immigration to Morocco occurred in the late
1920s, and brought mainly farmers and military men;
the second wave, mainly functionaries, arrived during and shortly after the Second World War. Obviously, there was a sharp difference in outlook between the older colon population and the newer arrivals. The "old Moroccan hands," *les vieux Marocains*, as they were called, had a more personal contact with the Moroccans themselves. Particularly in
the Sefrou region, where they had established the
first mechanized farms, they often knew Arabic,
worked closely with their Moroccan workers, and
were not cloistered in French ghettos. Their pater-

nalism was tempered by a kind of rugged indi-
vidualist approach. They had cleared the land, they
had turned scrub into well-tended and productive
farms, they "knew" the Moroccans and said that if
you trained them, they would work well. One had
the impression that Richard could have fit in with
these farmers, small entrepreneurs, and jacks-of-
all-trades. In any case, the remnants of this community by and large accepted him.

But Richard came to Morocco in 1950, as part of a
very different group of immigrants. These *nouveaux
vieux Marocains* as they were contemptuously called,
lived mainly in the great colon centers of Casablanca
and Meknes; they almost never knew Arabic, and
had little or no contact with the Moroccans outside
business hours. They saw themselves more in the
style of the insular colon in Oran or Algiers. Their ties
were to France and they were committed to a French
way of life. By the early fifties over 80 percent of the
French population in Morocco was living in major
cities. Moreover, they were mainly government
functionaries. The percentage of functionaries was
even higher than in the mother country. They were
not to sustain their presence for very long.

Richard sought the earlier identity but was overcome by the later one. He arrived when opportunities for the average Frenchman were closing
down, not opening up. Instead, he confronted an
active antagonism between the French and Moroccan communities. Richard was too weak to escape or
resist it. He found the now hardened lines between
the two communities too political to cross. Although
his personal dealings with the French community in
Morocco were always painful for him, he never

found a way either to integrate with them or free himself from them, because he was not courageous enough to defy the colon codes in any major way. Richard never learned Arabic. He repeatedly expressed a keen desire to do so, but he had mastered only a few words and phrases. What once would have been interpreted by the Moroccans as a welcome gesture from a newcomer might now, after eighteen years, seem mockingly insincere. Richard was clearly discouraged from following these impulses by the French community in Meknes, where he first settled, and by his wife, an Algerian colon, who boasted of her racial superiority. He was supportive of my fledgling efforts to learn Arabic. He asked me about methods, encouraged me and then would drift to a reverie about how he should have learned Arabic when he first arrived, how it would still be the thing to do, but *hélas,* his duties just would not permit it. Richard was truly a remnant of a dying colonialism, except that he had never reaped the earlier rewards.

Each morning Richard revved up his 1952 Ford and roared the kilometer and a half into Sefrou to pick up his supplies. As there were almost never any guests at l'Oliveraie this amounted to provisions for himself and his wife, the newspaper (*Le Petit Maro-cain*), and some wine. Except for a little passing contact with the storekeepers and exchanges of pleasantries with officials, Richard's world was restricted to the wino cab drivers, his wife, and two or three old French couples who accepted him as an equal. These last were people who had been in Morocco for forty years and had made niches for themselves as handymen or storekeepers. They respected the Moroc-

cans and lived essentially *en retraite*, both retired and
in retreat from contemporary France. There were
only a few of these gnarled, old Frenchmen left.
Richard observed each death with a sense of increas-
ing despair; each loss significantly eroded his world.

It has often been said that the worst of the parent
culture is exported with it, and this was certainly the
case for the young French residents I knew in
Morocco. In France one may choose between doing
military service or some alternate civilian service
overseas in the ex-colonies. Morocco had a severe
shortage of teachers for its bilingual school system
and has been forced to import large numbers of
French teachers to sustain it. Each year, therefore, a
score of young couples arrive in Sefrou to perform its
civilizing work. They are largely young bourgeois
who come to Morocco to avoid the barracks and to
live out fantasies not feasible for them in France.
They can afford villas, complete with gardens and
servants. Of equal importance is the fact that in
Morocco they can dominate. They dominate the servants, whom they treat with the obligatory patroniz-
ing condescension; and they dominate their students, whom they perceive as culturally inferior and
not truly worthy of the luxury of hope. Within their
own community they observe the old social distinctions and hierarchies of France, but with a new twist:
now they can play the leading roles.

Accordingly, they dominated and despised
Richard. There was a prescribed ritual which was
reenacted each year with a painful and predictable
regularity. As the new couples arrive in Sefrou they
stay first at L'Oliveraie while their affairs are being

arranged. Shortly they learn from more seasoned countrymen that l'Oliveraie is beneath them socially. At first, talking with Richard seems natural enough to them; he is an old hand, and he is French—one of their own in this foreign setting. Richard would repeat the same tired formulas and desperately try to create a relationship. There would be glimmerings, at times, but it never seemed to materialize. After these young couples had moved to the villas they might return to l'Oliveraie once, perhaps even twice, with their new acquaintances, but never more. The circle would close in the fall, as the new arrivals were ingested into the little community and told simply that Richard was "un pauvre type." His world was soon as impossibly distant from theirs as it would have been in Paris, except that in Sefrou there was little else for him.

Ironically enough, Richard began each fall with warnings about the Moroccans, their unpredictability and irrationality. He was trying to please, no longer knowing himself whether he believed his own stories, but feeling that the stories would fit the preconceived ideas of his new audience. In the first weeks they succumbed to their fears. Once settled in, however, such crass indulgence changed rather quickly to a more insidious rhetoric of "objectivity." They were there to educate the Third World. They liked the Moroccans, of course, they found them beautiful, exciting, and intriguing. But *les indigènes* simply could not do arithmetic. Despite the French efforts, the students just did not seem to learn. They were *sympa* but inferior. Richard was merely inferior.

Richard was actually quite lucid about the nature

of his situation, but he was absolutely incapable of changing it. He was in the wrong position at the wrong time. The hotel's decline fed itself; the more he lost on the hotel, the more the young French shunned him, the more the Moroccan functionaries refused his company, and the more dependent he became on the near alcoholic cab drivers, who were ostracized even by their own community. Each year one more of his circle died. The more he pressed the more strained his smile became, the more urgently he clung to the new arrivals the more surely he drove them away. Colonialism was dying, and neo-colonialism was taking its place.

I encouraged him to talk, and he was overjoyed. I spent many hours during those first few weeks listening to his stories. I was fluent in French and the entrée was immediate. The structural possibilities of the situation were also ideal for collecting information. I did not conceptualize it this way at the beginning, and for this reason (among others) I never systematically pursued this situation. I had come to Morocco intent on studying rural religion and politics. It seemed self-indulgent to be chatting with Richard about his past. One must be problem-oriented, my professors had insisted, and not be sidetracked by diversions, intriguing as they might seem. Further, one presumably risked being stigmatized by the local Muslim community.

Actually, I had been in a rather ideal "anthropological" position. I was fluent in the language, familiar with the culture, concerned with related issues, yet unquestionably an outsider—all by the fourth day in the country. With Richard I was not in a position of dominance or one of submission. I had access to

Richard as well as the younger French. The whole structure of the relations between them was easy to formulate and the needs of the various participants were such that they were in search of an outside observer to whom they could recount their troubles and reflections. I was in no position to threaten them, or to offer direct economic or political assistance. In retrospect, this climate was ideal for anthropological inquiry. At the time, its very ease and accessibility seemed to discount its potential value. Surely field-work required more toil.

The stillness of the hot afternoon, some two and a half months later, remains clearly in my memory. So does the emptiness of l'Oliveraie and the gloss of the wooden bar and its brass rim. Richard and I were chatting quietly with long pauses between remarks. He was in his habitual pose, bent over the bar, chin resting on his palm, as if preparing for an arm-wrestling match, the other arm jauntily placed on his hip. His eyes were opened wide with an eagerness still shining through. I was sitting, slightly hunched over, on a bar stool across from him.

Behind Richard, his art-deco radio was playing softly. The announcer said simply that Russian forces had invaded Czechoslovakia. Slowly, we exchanged pained glances but said nothing. The radio continued announcing details in an official tone thinly concealing excitement.

There was no turning back; I felt a horrified distance from my own civilization. The image of totalitarian armies smashing the Czechs again left me with a sense of decaying empires, cancerously destroying themselves.

2. Packaged Goods

The highway from Fez passes Richard's hotel and the edge of the medina proper before it turns into the Boulevard Mohammed V, named after the present king's father, an immensely popular leader. It then follows a sharp curve and gradual incline before it straightens out again to become the main thoroughfare for the new quarter of Sefrou. The lower boundary of the Ville Nouvelle is marked clearly by the boulevard, which is flanked by a park and a three-story arcaded set of buildings with shops on the ground floor and apartments above. Most of these shops offer a taste of progress—modern services, electric appliances, liquor, the post office and government bureaus. Immediately behind this thoroughfare is a section of small apartment houses which became the new center for the Jewish community of Sefrou, traditionally large and commercially important, as they left the crowded conditions of the *mellah* or enclosed Jewish quarter of the medina.

Behind this cluster of apartments lies the true Ville Nouvelle. The houses there are almost all single-family European style villas (imitation Swiss chalets, some with swimming pools) set behind luxuriant gardens replete with olive, fig, almond, pomegranate, and citrus trees. Recently a few single-family

houses have been built along modified Arabic patterns with an enclosed courtyard and if possible a
fountain.

The administration of the French Protectorate encouraged the preservation of what they considered
to be the traditional institutions of Morocco. The Protectorate was officially proclaimed in 1912 although
the complete pacification of the tribes was not accomplished until the mid-nineteen thirties. This
coincided roughly with the beginnings of the urban
nationalist movements which led to independence
for Morocco in 1956. The celebrated Marshal Lyautey
attempted to make Morocco into a progressive model
of colonial administration. Under his leadership the
cities of Morocco were not to be altered by the French
commercial, colon, and administrative presence. Instead, new cities, Villes Nouvelles, were to be constructed alongside the older towns. Throughout
Morocco one finds sometimes immediately adjacent
(as in the case of Sefrou), sometimes several kilometers distant (as with Fez or Marrakech), a European
city symbolized by the governmental buildings,
municipal parks, and broad avenues. Cities like Fez
and Sefrou still have no automobiles in the medina,
and the visual effect is one of two civilizations living
epochs apart, alongside one another. The symbolism
is deceiving; the social and cultural reality is quite
another story.

The Ville Nouvelle in Sefrou lies on the slopes
above the medina on land which was formerly orchards and gardens. This land belonged to the
people of the Klaa, a somewhat isolated quarter of
the medina. This quarter has a population density of

approximately 1300 people per hectare. For the medina as a whole, the figure is closer to 1100. The Ville Nouvelle has a density of 12 people per hectare. It is not entirely populated by the wealthy, however; some 50 percent of its residents were categorized as lower class in the 1960 census. These are either former landowners from the medina who retained their rights, relatives who have moved in with more successful cousins, or servants. But the wealthier and more powerful citizens of Sefrou live there also. The cultural tone is set by the French population. As we have seen, it is here that most of the "cooperants" settle in and play out their haute bourgeois fantasies. Their neighbors are the wealthier Moroccans who have adopted European patterns of dress and demeanor.

My first Arabic teacher was one of these merchants, a moderately prosperous, extremely hardworking and ambitious storekeeper, whom I shall call Ibrahim. The son of a mason, he and his younger brother operate a grocery store located under the arcade on the Boulevard Mohammed V. They cater mainly to the European population of Sefrou. They carry a variety of canned goods as well as magazines and newspapers which they bring in from Fez every day. They work hard and their money is not spent on conspicuous consumption but is saved and reinvested in the business or their property.

Ibrahim had begun his adult life by acting as a middleman between the French colonial administration and his fellow Moroccans. During the closing years of the Protectorate he had officially advanced to the post of government interpreter. He speaks

French quite well, though with an accent, but interestingly enough he has not been enticed or confused by the French literary and philosophic culture. He had correctly assessed the French as a possible resource to exploit commercially and he proceeded, in a modest fashion, to do so. The French language was an instrument which helped him reach his end. Ibrahim is an example of a class of Moroccans who have successfully played a mediating role between the French and their own community without succumbing to the debilitating identity confusion which usually accompanies the colonial presence. Ibrahim is not an intellectual, at least not a French-style intellectual. The Islamic reform movements in Morocco to which he belongs have helped him to avoid the corrosive acid of cultural doubt. Ibrahim has not abandoned his heritage. Quite the contrary, he has renewed it. His son learns both French and Classical Arabic. Ibrahim supports the mosque and the local parent-teacher association, which he helped found. He always struck me as an illustration of a person who had blended what social scientists refer to as tradition and modernity.

He had worked with Richard in the early days of Richard's stay in Sefrou. They were engaged in operating the town's movie theater together. The enterprise faltered after a period though, as Mrs. Richard refused to socialize with the Moroccans and Richard was regretfully forced into a fuller commitment to the hotel and his wife. Today Ibrahim and Richard exchange greetings, but that is all.

Ibrahim's younger brother had already done some work with another anthropologist who had been in

Sefrou several years earlier, and it was suggested that this might be a promising lead for me. After several days chez Richard, I became anxious to start learning Arabic and had talked to him and others about a possible teacher.

I was introduced to Ibrahim in his store on the Boulevard Mohammed V. Over a glass of mint tea, we politely and somewhat formally discussed the possibility of making arrangements to work together. He was quite straightforward with me, saying that he had not taught Moroccan before and therefore he could not promise that he would be good at it. He would try his best. Perhaps it would be wisest if we began on a trial basis. That way if it did not work out there would be no hard feelings. It would also not endanger his relations with the other foreigners in Sefrou. Of course, I understood and gratefully agreed. In closing he said that he was doing this favor because he was pleased that an American wanted to learn his language. He was proud of Arabic and proud of his heritage, he understood why I had come to Sefrou (to understand his society), and he would be glad to be of service. He would also be more than pleased to show me around the city whenever he had the time to do so. He sincerely hoped that I would be happy in Sefrou.

All of this turned out to be true. The weighed and modest evaluation of his abilities and intentions was quite just. The more usual rhetorical flourishes of self-aggrandizement and purity of intent, which play such an integral part in Moroccan forms of address, were absent from Ibrahim. He would have agreed with Ben Franklin that in business your words and reputation are your most valuable assets.

Ibrahim lived on the extreme edge of the Ville Nouvelle, at a point where the road was no longer paved. He had built himself a modified Arabic-style house with an enclosed courtyard which was the domain of his wife and mother. Vines and flowers were carefully arranged to grow over the courtyard providing shade and privacy. The interior of the house was furnished in a simple, almost ascetic fashion. The furniture consisted mainly of the typical urban style of low platforms with brocade covered pillows. A rule of thumb in determining the wealth of the owner of a house is the size of the pillows. This house, like its owner, was functional, restrained, and moderately prosperous.

Each morning during the summer I would trudge up the hill along the tree-lined road that winds through the villas arriving chez Ibrahim parched but eager. Our sessions lasted about six weeks and they gave me an object lesson, one of several I received, of how not to learn a language. Ibrahim was clearly concerned that Arabic be learned correctly and he spent many hours patiently preparing for our lessons. Unfortunately the two models of instruction available to him were distinctly unsuited to my personality and needs. The traditional Koranic methods of rote memorization were obviously out of the question. Therefore, quite naturally, Ibrahim made a valiant attempt to reduplicate the procedure through which he had learned French.

At first Ibrahim would come prepared with vocabulary lists which we would translate into French and then repeat to each other. So, for example, we would have a lesson on farm animals or rooms of the house, in comprehensive detail. The limits of this approach were soon apparent to both of us and we moved on to phrases. The phrases told a story, often about such things as ducks and ducklings, geese and goslings. I would leave Ibrahim's, trudge back to my room or to a cafe and work on the phrases and lists. Aside from the greetings which I learned readily and would use with confidence, it was frustrating and practically impossible to make use of phrases about farm animals or kitchen utensils. Ahmed, the waiter, had by now warmed up considerably and was clearly pleased by my efforts. We would enthusiastically exchange greetings when I returned there, but there was little to sustain us beyond that. Desire alone does not yield conversation.

After a month or so I realized what the problem was. Ibrahim was directly translating the phrases and exercises in his old French grammar book into Arabic. What I was getting was a series of retranslated lessons, ready for export, but next to useless for dealing with Moroccan life. In other circumstances I might have struggled along with that approach for months but my state of eager anticipation and the lack of progress yielded geometrically spiralling anxiety. For a month or so I internalized the situation: I was just not good at languages, Ibrahim was being so clearly conscientious and open; it was my fault; Arabic is a difficult language, and so on. My next reaction was anger, both at Ibrahim and myself. Absurd. It was not a problem of personalities. The structure of the situation itself was standing in the way. That had to be changed.

Ibrahim had turned his position as an intermediary between the European and Moroccan communities into a profession. He was a packager and transmitter of commodities and services, a middleman, a government translator of official messages. He was packaging Arabic for me as if it were a tourist brochure. He was willing to orient me to the fringes of the Moroccan community, to the Ville Nouvelle of Moroccan culture, but there was a deep resistance on his part to any further penetration.

Jacques Berque has spoken of language, women, and religion as the three domains of freedom in which North Africans had most fiercely resisted European transgression. Once the economic domination and control of the land had been accomplished these domains were even more highly cathected and symbolically charged realms of integrity and identity. Even here, of course, European penetration could not be stopped completely, but only circumvented. Thus, for example, armies of prostitutes are found in many North African cities, but there was almost no intermarriage between European men and North African women. A form of public Islam veiled the brotherhoods, sects, and myriad other forms of religious practice which proliferated beyond the reach of French control. The Arabic language also had to be protected. Aside from the obvious material and technological advantages of learning French, the large response can also be interpreted as a defensive action to keep the French away from Arabic. As we have seen, whereas the early colon community in Morocco often did learn some Arabic, the second wave of immigrants almost never did. By then enough Moroccans had learned enough French.

The difficulties with Ibrahim were connected to this. I resented his reading of my intentions. That none of this was formulated in these terms during the six weeks or so I worked with Ibrahim goes without saying. But the resistances and lack of progress was clear enough. My goals and his were essentially contradictory. He was presenting me with surfaces and packaged facets. This was unsatisfactory. His resistance was polite but firm. Ultimately, I respected it. One could make his emergent world of petit bourgeois neo-traditionalism a focus of study, and other anthropologists have. But it didn't suit my temperament, and it was not what I had come to Morocco to discover. Therefore, I had to find other situations.

About this time, two friends from America came to visit me, and we decided to go to Marrakech for several days. I mentioned this to Ibrahim and he said he would like to come along. He had cousins in Marrakech whom he would like to visit, and he would be happy to act as our guide. I was not enthusiastic about the idea since I had been looking forward to the trip as a relief from the mounting anxiety of learning Arabic. Bringing my teacher along hardly seemed a vacation. But, he had been so hospitable and generous with me that I could hardly say no.

Things went smoothly at first. On the second morning, Ibrahim announced not only that he had no relatives in Marrakech but that he had unfortunately forgotten to bring along enough money to pay for his room. This was one of my first direct experiences of Otherness. Ibrahim was simply testing the limits of the situation. Within Moroccan culture this is a standardized and normal thing to do, as I was to find out. He was pushing to see if I would pay for his trip. When, after much confusion and uncertainty on my part, I refused (mainly because I lacked the money at the time) Ibrahim backed down and produced his wallet. He was maximizing his resources, exploiting the situation economically, proceeding as he had in the past. We had been working together for over a month and he now felt that he could push our contractual limits more in his favor. The point is not that Ibrahim was greedy or calculating. Greed or any of the other venal sins were in ample supply back home. What was upsetting was the realization that I had been engaged with this man every day for well over a month, we had spent many hours talking French together in addition to the Arabic lessons, and I had proceeded to "typify" him. But my typifications were fundamentally incorrect and ethnocentric. Basically I had been conceiving of him as a friend because of the seeming personal relationship we had established. But Ibrahim, a lot less confusedly, had basically conceptualized me as a resource. He was not unjustly situating me with the other Europeans with whom he had dealings. I had gone into anthropology in search of Otherness. Meeting it on an experiential level was a shock which caused me to begin fundamental reconceptualization about social and cultural categories. Presumably this was the sort of thing I had come to Morocco to find, yet every time these breaks occurred they were upsetting.

One could construct smooth and seemingly conflict-free modes of interaction with people (during the course of many hours of trivial conversation) which would suddenly break down. One assumes in everyday life, when it goes smoothly, that people share what has been called a life-world—certain primary assumptions about the nature of the social world, about social personae, about how events occur and more or less what they imply. This fabric of meaning, which is a necessary underpinning for all cultures, enables actors to proceed from day to day and hour to hour without having to reconstruct social relations from scratch (each time they meet) or engage in discussions of semantics (every time they wish to chat). Within a culture most of these articulations from gesture to larger significance, from patter to values, can be taken for granted because they are largely shared. It has been pointed out that common sense is "thin"—loosely articulated, largely taken for granted, incapable of withstanding sustained scrutiny. My misunderstanding with Ibrahim points up this thinness. Common sense, everyday interaction always implies more than itself. Ibrahim and I were from different cultures, and the implications which we drew in Marrakech about daily life were leagues apart.

3. Ali: An Insider's Outsider

Just outside the walls of the medina, perhaps two hundred yards down a slight hill from the Boulevard Mohammed V and across from the municipal park, lies an open area. It was here that the French concentrated their marketing and commercial activities. Sefrou had traditionally been an important depot for the rural tribes and nearby town, but under the Protectorate its scope and importance were systematized and enlarged in order to increase commerce, taxation, and political stability. A large dirt courtyard set between a low arcaded set of buildings serves as a kind of wholesale vegetable market. Nearby, up some steps, adjacent to Sefrou's thick walls, an area is reserved for craft goods such as woven mats. When the market is not operating, it serves as a playground and miniature soccer field. On the outskirts of the town, rural Berbers gather on Thursdays at the animal market, an enclosed lot with a tax collector at its gates. Rain or shine, animated and serious bargaining takes place. The sale of even one sheep for a poor Berber may represent a transaction he has been anticipating for several months.

As one enters the large gates of the medina, traditionally shut at night for security reasons, one leaves the Cartesian avenues, neat arcades, and open spaces which the French have contributed to Sefrou. The clearest reference point is the river, Wed Aggai,

31

which rambles through the center of the medina. In
1950 it had overflown its banks during a devastating
flash flood, and its channel had been redug so it now
flows by in an almost subterranean fashion. Far
below one hears the chatter of women as they wash
their clothes in the river.

Except when following the river, one has to learn
one's way around the medina through habit and
practice. No straight streets extend for any distance;
the only distinctive section of the medina is the
walled mellah, or Jewish quarter, which like the medina itself has large gates controlling the only available approach to it, a short bridge. Today most of the
Jews have left Sefrou altogether or moved out of the
mellah into the more modern sections of the city.
Only poor and newly arrived countrymen now join
the population of prostitutes as inhabitants of the
mellah.

There are several named quarters in the medina,
but the residential patterns of Sefrou can only be
characterized by their heterogeneity. Aside from the
mellah in former times, there is no single area which
is markedly homogenous as to ethnic group, as to
rural versus urban origin, or as to occupational
categories. Some of the richest families live in ram-
bling compounds immediately adjacent to the dwellings of poor, rural countrymen looking for work.
Recently, many of the more prosperous have relo-
cated in newer quarters of Sefrou. But even there,
there is no clear correlation between wealth, ethni-
city, occupation, or class. The medina is densely
populated with over 40 percent of Sefrou's population living on 2.2 percent of the land.

I had been given the names, by anthropologists

who previously worked in Sefrou, of two men who might serve as informants for my research. These two were habitually found in the one true moorish style cafe remaining in the medina, located not far from the main mosque and the river. Just ask anyone, I was told, and they will direct you there. At the heart of the old city, one of the few true intersections, was indeed a cafe. It was in a rather decrepit state, with the tiles sorely in need of repair, the tables battered and shaky, and the inhabitants bedraggled. A few men were playing cards with animated gestures, while others simply sat clutching their glass teacups. I asked in French, following a few broken Arabic greetings, for the owner. After an auspicious silence he appeared and greeted me warmly. He said in halting French that I was welcome in Morocco, that he was at my service, that if there was anything I needed I should come to him, and that his son spoke French and he would send for him. Finally, he insisted that I stay in his cafe.

As this very public exchange was taking place on the threshold of the cafe, a tall, lanky man with a big smile came darting out of a store across the narrow square and entered with a series of effusive greetings. He shook hands with the cafe owner, who seemed at best mildly pleased to see him, and told me about the same thing as the first man had, though in an abbreviated version, since his French was minimal. This must be Ali, the man from Sidi Lahcen Lyussi, the religious center. He was supposed to be a curer of sorts, an excellent informant (patient, intelligent, curious, imaginative), all too happy to work for money and a marvelous guide to Sefrou and its hinterlands.

I accepted the tea but explained that I would not stay because I had an appointment with Ibrahim; could I come back tomorrow? *Waxxa, waxxa*—of course. Chronic underemployment and the consequent surplus of spare time are unfortunately of aid to the anthropologist's endeavor. Many of the men in the medina worked only sporadically, and were ready to pursue any potential source of money. They were also curious, and eager for a new distraction. The anthropologist offered the possibility of both.

I came back the next morning and found Ali across the street sitting in front of a small clothing store. The store was owned by a roly-poly friend of his known as Soussi. Literally, Soussi means a man from the Sous region of Southern Morocco, famous for its frugal shopkeepers, who have spread out to all the major regions in Morocco. This Soussi, it turns out, was neither hardworking, thrifty, nor dour. He was almost always eager to close his shop and go off on a walk or an adventure, treating his business obligations like an annoyance.

When I arrived, several women were making a vain attempt to bargain Soussi down on a scarf, but he lost interest and chased them away, much to their amazement. Ali greeted me warmly, pulled up another rickety chair, and called across the way for two glasses of sweet mint tea. Much of the population of Sefrou, or so it seemed, careened past us. The intersection lay at a juncture of three curving slopes, so that people, donkeys, dogs, and sheep would suddenly appear from around a corner accelerating into the little square and then go off again around the bend or up the other side in a roller-coaster motion. Ali and Soussi seemed to know practically everyone who passed by. Quick and cursory welcomes were exchanged in rapid spit-fire fashion as the voice and its owner disappeared around the bend. As a New Yorker and a devotee of street life, I felt much more at ease here than in the formal and quasi-suburban atmosphere of the Ville Nouvelle. In addition, it was immensely "ethnographic" and fulfilled all of my images of myself as anthropologist sitting in the heart of a thousand-year-old walled city with my turbaned friends, notebook on my lap, drinking tea and being the participant observer.

As the morning passed the tea kept coming. Tea and sugar have a tyrannical and almost obsessive centrality in Morocco. Its preparation and consumption are daily rituals of generosity and exchange, but it is also economically a heavy load to bear. Who pays for how much of the tea and sugar, who owes whom from the other day or last week, and the quality of the ingredients are all constant themes of everyday life. As much as 40 percent of a poor peasant's cash income can be spent on tea and sugar. One gets the impression that tea must be one of the oldest and most stable of Moroccan staples, but this is not the case. In the rural areas around Sefrou, it can be shown that tea and sugar have been systematically substituted for protein over the last seventy or eighty years. Actually, tea was introduced into Morocco by the English in the eighteenth century, and its use did not become widespread until the nineteenth. It was only during the crisis years of 1874-1884 that tea became the national drink in Morocco. Consumption

Ali and friends: Sefrou demi-monde.

tripled during that decade, and sugar was close behind; German, French, and English companies systematically developed a market whose extent they must have been surprised to discover.

In any case, tea is now a cherished part of Moroccan life. Its preparation—the careful breaking of the cones of sugar with a little hammer, the washing and handling of the pot, the apportionment of the tea and mint, its slow bubbling watched over with great care and attention by all concerned, its sampling, reheating, and resampling, its inevitable re-sweetening—and finally its triumphant pouring through the long curved spout of the kettle was a scene I was to witness hundreds of times during my stay.

A Berber woman, dressed in gaudy colored clothes with a very small baby strapped on her back, appeared from around the bend. She exchanged a few words with Ali and bent over. Ali took the head of the baby, who could not have been more than a few months old, firmly in his hands. Putting his mouth to the child's mouth he swiftly and with great assurance made a quick sucking noise. The baby began to howl. With an air of professional pride Ali showed the mother some spittle containing a black speck. She seemed satisfied, gave him a few coins, and left.

The completely casual way in which Ali had performed this act was stunning in its simplicity. The shifting of perspectives, almost without a pause, was eye-opening. The whole scenario was taken for granted by Ali, Soussi, and the woman. Only the baby and the anthropologist were disturbed by it. I recovered my composure quickly enough, and noted that I had identified a curing practice.

Fieldwork is a dialectic between reflection and immediacy. Both are cultural constructs. Our scientific categories help us to recognize, describe, and develop areas of inquiry. But one cannot engage in questioning and redefining twenty-four hours a day. The scientific perspective on the world is hard to sustain. In the field there is less to fall back on; the world of everyday life changes more rapidly and dramatically than it would at home. There is an accelerated dialectic between the recognition of new experiences and their normalization.

As I began to question Ali about the curing, my scientific categories were modified—I understood more about curing, its tacit assumptions, modes of action, and limits—but my common-sense world was also changed. I knew no curers in New York. Thus the first time I witnessed activities like this one they required greatly heightened attention on my part; they focussed and dominated my consciousness. But as the fieldwork progressed and I witnessed such performances a number of times, I began to take them largely for granted. They increasingly became part of my stock of knowledge, part of my world. Ali's curing activity no longer jolted my consciousness, and I was free to focus elsewhere.

This highlighting, identification, and analysis also disturbed Ali's usual patterns of experience. He was constantly being forced to reflect on his own activities and objectify them. Because he was a good informant, he seemed to enjoy this process and soon began to develop an art of presenting his world to me. The better he became at it, the more we shared together. But the more we engaged in such activity, the more he experienced aspects of his own life in new ways. Under my systematic questioning, Ali was taking realms of his own world and interpreting them for an outsider. This meant that he, too, was spending more time in this liminal, self-conscious world between cultures. This is a difficult and trying experience—one could almost say it is "unnatural"—and not everyone will tolerate its ambiguities and strains.

This was the beginning of the dialectic process of fieldwork. I say dialectic because neither the subject nor the object remain static. With Richard or Ibrahim, there had been only minor movement on either side. But with Ali there began to emerge a mutually constructed ground of experience and understanding, a realm of tenuous common sense which was constantly breaking down, being patched-up, and re-examined, first here, then there.

This examination, although grounded in and constantly mediated by everyday experience of this new sort, is governed for the anthropologist by his professional concerns. Ultimately this constitutes his commitment; this is why he is there. For the informant, it is a more practical affair, both in the sense that we can assume that his motivations are primarily pragmatic and in the sense that he is developing a practical art of response and presentation.

As time wears on, anthropologist and informant share a stock of experiences upon which they hope to rely with less self-reflection in the future. The common understanding they construct is fragile and thin, but it is upon this shaky ground that anthropological inquiry proceeds.

*   *   *

Ali promised to take me to a wedding in the village of Sidi Lahcen Lyussi. I had already been to several urban weddings. The best Moroccan food, music, and ceremonial were displayed on these occasions. It was a nice change of pace, a break in the routine. The wedding would be an excellent opportunity for me to see the village, and for the villagers to see me.

That afternoon, Ali came by. I told him I wasn't sure I would be able to go with him because I was suffering from a stomach virus. The prospect of being in a strange and demanding situation where I wanted to please, for such a long period, seemed overwhelming, especially in my present condition. Ali expressed keen disappointment at this. He had clearly counted on transportation in my car and the mixed prestige of arriving with the most auspicious guest (if not the guest of honor).

When he returned the next day I was feeling a bit better. He assured me that we would stay only for a short time. He stressed all the preliminary politicking and arranging he had done; if I didn't show up it would not be good for either of us. So I agreed, but made him promise me that we would stay only an hour or so because I was still weak. He repeated his promise several times saying we would leave whenever I felt like it.

Ali and Soussi came to my house around nine that evening and we were off. I was already somewhat tired and repeated clearly to Soussi, a renowned partygoer in his own right, that we would stay only for a short time and then return to Sefrou. *Waxxa,* O.K.?

It was already growing dark as we left Sefrou. By the time we turned off the highway onto the unpaved road which leads to the village, it was nearly pitch black, depriving me of a sense of the countryside, while adding to my feelings of uncertainty about the whole affair. Nonetheless, on arriving in the village I was exhilarated.

The wedding itself was held in a set of connected houses which formed a compound. A group of sons had built simple mud and mortar houses next to each other as they married, and by now these formed an enclosed compound. Each part of the enclosure was made up of a two-story building. The facilities for the animals and cooking areas were downstairs, the sleeping quarters were on the top level, connected by a rickety staircase. That night the center of the compound area had been covered with straw for the dancing. We were welcomed and ushered up the stairs into a long narrow room furnished with thin cushions along the perimeters. Perhaps five tables were arranged parallel to each other, running the length of the room. I told myself it was a good thing we had come, a wise decision. Everyone was friendly and seemed to know who I was. We had tea, then after perhaps an hour of chatting and banter, dinner was served on battered but polished metal trays. The hour of talk had passed amicably enough, even though my minimal Arabic did not permit much expansive conversation. I still had a beard at this point, and there was much friendly but insistent joking that this was improper for such a young man. The dinner was simple but nicely prepared, consisting of goat meat in a sort of olive oil stew with freshly baked bread, still warm from the oven.

"*Much time is spent hanging around cafes drinking tea.*"

After we ate and drank more tea, we went down to the courtyard, where the dancing began. I watched from a corner, leaning against a pillar. The dancers were all men, of course, and they formed two lines facing each other, their arms draped over one another's shoulders. Between the two lines was a singer with a crude tambourine. He sang and swayed back and forth. The lines of men responded in turn to his direct, insistent beat, answering his verses with verses of their own. The women were peeping out from another part of the compound where they had eaten their dinner. They were all dressed in their best clothes, brightly colored kaftans. They answered the various verses with calls of their own, enthusiastically urging the men on. Since I did not understand the songs and was not dancing, my excitement wore off rapidly. Ali was one of the most dedicated of the dancers, and it was difficult to catch his attention. During a break when the central singer was warming his tambourine over the fire to restretch the skin, I finally got Ali's ear and told him politely but insistently that I was not feeling well, that we had been here three hours already. It was midnight, could we leave soon after the next round of dances maybe? Of course, he said, just a few more minutes, no problem, don't worry, I understand.

An hour later I tried again and received the same answer. This time, however, I was getting angrier and more frustrated; I was feeling truly ill. The mountain air was quite cold by now, and I had not dressed warmly enough. I felt entirely at Ali's mercy. I didn't want to antagonize him, but neither did I want to stay. I continued to grumble to myself but managed to smile at whoever was smiling at me.

Finally, at three in the morning, I could stand it no longer. I was feeling terrible. I was furious at Ali but loath to express it. I was going to leave, regardless of the consequences. I told Soussi, let's go; if you want a ride, get Ali and that's it. Ali at this point was nowhere in sight. Soussi went off and returned to the car with a smiling and contented Ali. I was warming the engine up, publicly announcing my readiness to leave. They climbed in, Soussi in the front and Ali in the back, and we were off. The road for the first five miles is little more than a path—untarred, pitted, and winding and steep in places. I was a novice driver and unsure of myself, so I said nothing, concentrating all my energy on staying on the road and keeping the car going. I managed to negotiate this stretch of road successfully and heaved a sigh of relief when we reached the highway.

Soussi had been keeping up a steady flow of chatter as we bumped over the country road. I had kept my silence, ignoring Ali in the back, who said little himself. When we reached the highway and began rolling smoothly toward Sefrou, he asked in a nonchalant manner, *wash ferhan?*, are you happy? I snickered and said no. He pursued this. Why not? In simple terms I told him that I was sick, that it was three-thirty in the morning, and all I wanted to do was go home to bed—adding that I sincerely hoped he had enjoyed himself. Yes, he said, he had enjoyed himself, but if I was unhappy then the whole evening was spoiled, he was getting out of the car. Please, Ali, I said, let's just get back to Sefrou in peace. But why are you unhappy? I reminded him of his promise. If you are unhappy, he said, then I will talk back. This exchange was repeated several times, Soussi's vain attempts at mediation being ignored by both sides. Finally I told Ali he was acting like a baby, and yes, I was unhappy. He never offered any specific excuses but only insisted that if I was unhappy he would walk. He started to lean over and open the door on Soussi's side, scaring Soussi witless. We were traveling at forty miles an hour, and it scared me too, and I slowed down to ten. He challenged me again asking me if I was happy. I just could not bring myself to answer yes. My superego told me I should. But the events of the evening combined with the frustration of not being able to express myself fully to him in Arabic got the better of me. After another exchange and bluff on his part, I stopped the car to let him get out, which he now had to do. He did, promptly, and began striding down the dark highway in the direction of Sefrou. I let him get about one hundred yards ahead and then drove up alongside and told him to get in the car. He looked the other way. Soussi tried his luck with the same results. We repeated this melodrama two more times. I was confused, nauseous, and totally frustrated. I stepped on the gas and off we went to Sefrou, leaving Ali to walk the remaining five miles.

I went to sleep immediately, but woke from a fitful night saying to myself that I had probably made a grave professional mistake, because the informant is always right. Otherwise I was unrepentant. It was quite possible that I had ruined my relationship with Ali and that I had done irreparable damage to my chances of working my way into the village. But there were other things worth studying in Morocco, and it was something I would just have to make the best of. I took a walk through the tree-lined streets of the Ville Nouvelle and remembered a story a friend had told me before we took our doctoral exams; he had had nightmares for a week before the exams in which he saw himself as a shoe salesman. I mentally tried several occupations on for size as I drifted aimlessly among the villas. I felt calm; if this was anthropology and if I had ruined it for myself, then it simply wasn't for me.

The parameters seemed clear enough. I had to clarify for myself where I stood. If the informant was always right, then by implication the anthropologist had to become a sort of non-person, or more accurately a total persona. He had to be willing to enter into any situation as a smiling observer and carefully note down the specifics of the event under consideration. If one was interested in symbolic analysis or expressive culture, then the more elusive dimensions of feeling tone, gesture, and the like would be no exception. This was the position my professors had advocated: one simply endured whatever inconveniences and annoyances came along. One had to completely subordinate one's own code of ethics, conduct, and world view, to "suspend disbelief," as another colleague was proud of putting it, and sympathetically and accurately record events.

All of this had seemed simple enough back in Chicago (where, more accurately, no one paid more than lip service to these problems), but it was far from simple at the wedding. Ali had been a steady companion during the previous month and I had established a real rapport with him, more as a friend than as an informant; I was getting acclimated to Sefrou, and my Arabic was still too limited for us to do any sustained and systematic work together. I found the demands of greater self-control and abnegation hard to accept. I was used to engaging people energetically and found the idea of a year constantly on my guard, with very little to fall back on except the joys of asceticism, productive sublimation, and the pleasures of self-control, a grim prospect.

By refusing at least tacitly to acknowledge the existence and validity of fundamental Moroccan values, one skews the knowledge one collects. The informant has not stopped living his life, and has not willingly suspended his fundamental assumptions. This is not an equal relationship—after all, the informant has only the foggiest notion of what this strange foreigner is really after. For the rest of the day, the informant returns to his own life, perhaps slightly troubled by the cloud of the anthropologist's questions or the taunts of his comrades. But as confidence is built up, the informant judges and interacts with the anthropologist in his own habitual style, even if the outsider status is never eliminated.

As the explicit self-consciousness of the unnaturalness of the situation declines (it is never altogether absent), the implicit modes of action and judgment of both sides return. The anthropologist is supposed to be aware of this and to control himself. The informant is simply supposed to "be himself."

At the wedding Ali was beginning to test me, much in the way that Moroccans test each other to ascertain strengths and weaknesses. He was pushing and probing. I tried to avoid responding in the counter-assertive style of another Moroccan, vainly offering instead the persona of anthropologist, all-accepting. He continued to interpret my behavior in his own terms: he saw me as weak, giving in to each of his testing thrusts. So the cycle continued: he would probe more deeply, show his dominance, and exhibit my submission and lack of character. Even on the way back to Sefrou he was testing me, and in what was a backhanded compliment, trying to humiliate me. But Ali was uneasy with his victories, and shifted to defining the situation in terms of a guest-host relationship. My silence in the car clearly signaled the limits of my submission. His response was a strong one: Was I happy? Was he a good host?

The role of the host combines two of the most important of Moroccan values. As throughout the Arabic world, the host is judged by his generosity. The truly good host is one whose bounty, the largesse he shows his guests, is truly never-ending. One of the highest compliments one can pay to a man is to say that he is *karim*, generous. The epitome of the host is the man who can entertain many people and distribute his bounty graciously. This links him ultimately to Allah, who is the source of bounty.

If the generosity is accepted by the guest, then a very clear relationship of domination is established. The guest, while being fed and taken care of, is by that very token acknowledging the power of the host. Merely entering into such a position represents an acceptance of submission. In this fiercely egalitarian society, the necessity of exchange or reciprocity so as to restore the balance is keenly felt. Moroccans will go to great lengths, and endure rather severe personal privation, to reciprocate hospitality. By so doing, they reestablish their claim to independence.

Later in the day, I went down to Soussi's store in search of Ali to try and make amends. At first he refused even to shake hands, and was suitably haughty. But with the aid of Soussi's mediation and innumerable and profuse apologies on my part, he began to come round. By the time I left them later that afternoon it was clear that we had reestablished our relationship. Actually, it had been broadened by the confrontation. I had in fact acknowledged him. I had, in his own terms, pulled the rug out from under him—first by cutting off communication and then by challenging his gambit in the car. There was a fortuitous congruence between my breaking point and Moroccan cultural style. Perhaps in another situation my behavior might have proved irreparable. Brinkmanship, however, is a fact of everyday life in Morocco, and finesse in its use is a necessity. By finally standing up to Ali I had communicated to him.

Indeed, from that point on, we got along famously. It was only after this incident that he began to reveal to me two aspects of his life which he had previously concealed: his involvement in an ecstatic brotherhood, and his involvement in prostitution.

*   *   *

Religious brotherhoods have played a prominent role in Moroccan history. Today, a great number of different types are found in Morocco, ranging from several local adepts of a holy man to the much larger and more powerful brotherhoods with adherents in the Middle East and Africa. Most of these Moroccan brotherhoods trace their origins to a powerful saint from whom they claim their divine power, their *baraka*. Religious power, as most other things in Morocco, tends to be personalized and manifests itself through particularly forceful individuals, whose spiritual strength may take many forms, ranging from scholastic learning to curative powers to great feats of spiritual or physical endurance. Once a man has manifested his *baraka* in the world (and it is socially recognized) he will often attract a set of devotees who will follow his "path" in the hope of attaining some of his divine grace. A legend frequently grows up around his purported deeds, and if his descendants are canny enough, a line of succession which controls the divine power may be established.

Alternately, the holiness of the saint my be transmitted by the leaders of a brotherhood's lodge rather than genealogically. These lodges vary a great deal as to the nature of their practices and self-conception. On the one extreme are some of the reformist urban lodges in Fez, sober and restrained bourgeois groups defending what they consider to be the pure orthodoxy of Islam against the excesses of their countrymen. Like other Islamic reform movements, they are strongly opposed to saint worship, ecstatic behavior, trance, and all practices which to them are non-Koranic corruptions of the faith.

On the other end of the spectrum are the brotherhoods which the French characteristically referred to as the *confreries populaires*. These peoples' brotherhoods, usually grouped under the generic name of

Sufi, are not concerned with orthodoxy per se, but rather seek immediate access to spiritual power. Two of the most famous of these brotherhoods—the Aissawa and the Hamadcha—are directly concerned with curing. They first gained prominence in the sixteenth and seventeenth centuries, a period of prolonged religious and political turbulence. They have become famous for their spectacular methods, such as head-slashing, fire-eating, and snake-charming.

These two brotherhoods draw a large proportion of their membership from the urban poor, although they do have many rural adherents. It should be emphasized that many Moroccans belong to more than one brotherhood, access to the divine is not a closed corporate activity. Membership in several brotherhoods which take radically different approaches is not seen as a contradiction. It seems to be only the highly self-conscious reformers who are troubled by this. Most Moroccans are not. Here, as elsewhere in Morocco, options are maximized and neat sociological correlations are undercut by the fluidity of the culture.

The brotherhoods themselves are loosely organized. There is a local head, the *moqaddem* (literally, "he who stands in front") who is charged with taking care of daily affairs, collecting and distributing alms, organizing and directing the activities of the brotherhood, and serving as a mediator for disputes. He is not chosen by the national brotherhood but by the local members. He is usually a man who is both spiritually meritorious and politically astute.

Membership is also a fairly casual affair. There are no special initiation rites, no secret instruction, and no elaborate hierarchy among the members. The path or litany of the brotherhood, its *dikr*, is usually very simple, often a variant on the name or attributes of Allah, repeated endlessly. There is no formal membership in most brotherhoods. Those who participate regularly will have the most influence in daily affairs, but everyone is welcome. Kinship or genealogical strictures may be present for some of the official positions, but they play a relatively minor role, and in any case genealogical manipulation is standard practice in Morocco.

Ali was a member of the Aissawa brotherhood, which traces its spiritual genealogy back to Sidi ben Aissa, who, as far as historical research has been able to establish, lived in the late fifteenth century. Popular legend, however, places him in the seventeenth century at the time of the founding of the current dynasty. Be that as it may, Sidi ben Aissa's legend concentrates on the fabulous curative powers which he is said to have possessed and his extraordinary ability to tame wild creatures, particularly poisonous snakes. These traits mark the Aissawa activities today.

The fact that Ali was a descendant of a saint who spent a good part of his career opposing brotherhoods such as the Aissawa is not seen as a paradox. In fact, his role as *wlad siyyed*, the descendant of a saint, enhanced his spiritual reputation among the devotees of the Aissawa. This was confirmed by the warm and hearty greetings which met Ali at the door of a house not far from the main mosque in the center of Sefrou where a "night" was going to be performed for a sick boy. Ali had told the members that I was coming, and there was little fuss as we entered. The people seemed preoccupied. The only comment beyond the usual greetings came from a woman who noticed that I was wearing a maroon jacket and suggested to Ali that I remove it before going into the other room, since this might be dangerous. At their celebration each year in Meknes, which honors their patron saint, bystanders have been attacked by crowds of adepts who spot a red shirt or tie. I gladly took it off.

There were two main rooms. The smaller one was a sort of anteroom where various implements and props needed for the "night" were stored: several charcoal burners, torches, kerosene, and a carton of poisonous snakes. From this room we could see into the main and much larger room where the curing activities of the night would take place.

For the first hour or so that we were there, some fifteen men danced to the beat of three tambourines while chanting the *dikr* or litany of the brotherhood, which was essentially the name of Allah. The dancing was done in a line facing the musicians, in a five-against-one then three-against-one rhythm, repeated and repeated and repeated. Hands were held joined at waist level, the dancers swaying to the beat in a circular movement which carried the wave-like motion in counterpoint to the swaying of their hips. Heads were rolled elliptically from side to side. This very peaceful and graceful movement was occasionally punctuated when one of the dancers would come out in front of the line, only to continue the dance in essentially the same loose style. Later on in the evening as several of the dancers became possessed, the line softened into an enclosure. Graceful, contrapuntal motions highlighted the mood of protective intimacy.

The dancers ranged from adolescent boys and girls to one man who must have been eighty. Although during the course of the "night" there were several women dancers, the event lacked an orchestrated form. When possessed, women emerged from the audience to dance next to the men. Their dances tended to be more excited and jagged, with violent twirling of the hair (now unbraided), often ending with a dramatic collapse.

The whole evening was kept in hand by the watchful eye of one man, the *moqaddem*. He kept the chanting going, made sure that the dancers who became possessed did not hurt themselves, and gently ushered them off to the arms of women waiting to wash their faces and soothe them. Later on he also kept a close eye on all involved to prevent severe accidents from occurring. His manner was very off-stage and directorial, quite un-Moroccan in tone and procedure.

After several hours of this rhythmic chanting, interrupted only by the need to reheat the tambourine skins or by the staccato bursts of possession (all of which I found to be extremely relaxing and comforting), the *moqaddem* lit the charcoal burners and a sequence of fire-eating began. He doused a set of torches with what appeared to be kerosene and then presented them to each of the swaying dancers, who were still in line formation. The rhythm was constant. But now each dancer held a blazing torch under his gown, *djelleba*, then slowly circled his hair with it, and finally jabbed it provocatively at his mouth. Each of these sets seemed to last several minutes, until the torches would go out. Then there was a short break, the *moqaddem* would relight the torches, and the sequence would begin again. They gradually moved to a scenario in which the line dancing continued but this time each man in turn would dance out in front and perform the routine with the blazing torch. The *moqaddem* kept a close eye on these procedures, concerned lest a dancer go too deeply into trance, collapse on the floor, and burn himself. When he thought that one of the men had danced enough he would simply say *eh-wah* (well?), and the man would hand him the torch and return modestly to the line. This night Ali did not eat the fire. He said that he had just attended a "night" and was still too exhausted to do it again. The standardized movement of the torch around the head, clothes, and mouth seemed to drain off a great deal of emotional energy.

After the fire sequences the intensity of the evening seemed to drop off, although the swaying and chanting continued. Some time later, Ali danced out in front of the line, quite deep in trance, and rolling up his sleeve, gracefully and rhythmically slashed his forearms with his fingernails. Although that night his arms were covered with blood, the next day he mysteriously had only minor scratches. He was thoroughly exhausted and dispirited, and complained of a severe headache.

The climax of the evening was the curing ceremonial, which came toward midnight. The first several hours of dancing were not specifically aimed at curing, although the deep psychic involvement of the dancers was clear. The "night" was being held for a young boy. His family sponsored the night, which essentially meant providing the house and feeding the guests, which was a significant expense for such a poor family.

Five men took over the center of the floor and four of them proceeded to make growling noises like lions, mimicking their actions. The fifth man went into the adjoining room and returned with the little boy in his arms. Were it not for the growling, I could best describe what followed as a highly stylized and exquisitely executed mime. The four "lions" pan-tomimed attacks on the boy and his guardian, only to be warded off by the guardian's counter-thrusts, all of this languidly carried out. The whole performance was powerfully convincing. The use of space, in expanding and contracting circles, was beautifully choreographed. The power of the dance was heightened by the passing of the boy from man to man. As each man received the sick boy he would smoothly and totally transform his gestures from those of an attacking and growling lion into those of a protective and cuddling guardian. The whole form of the mime-dance was gentle variations of expansion and contraction, attack and defense, all in the sleep-walking movements of deep trance.

The "night" ended with all the members sitting around the *moqaddem*, who was given a tambourine and the Aissawa flag. He led them in a final chant. Weary and drained, the dancers snapped out of their revery and the "night" was over. Food was served but there was little energy left to enjoy it. There was some perfunctory talk during the meal and we left shortly thereafter. Ali remarked the next day that the boy was apparently better. We knew, however, that these "nights" were essentially psychotherapeutic for all concerned, and would no doubt have to be repeated in a few months.

Perhaps the most surprising thing to me about the night was how totally natural it seemed. Both at the time and in retrospect, it had the same deeply calming and cathartic effect for me as seeing John Coltrane perform. In both cases, polished performers worked in and elaborated a cultural form in which they could explore feelings and troubled states of mind. Through this form they discovered and communicated a measure of release. The sweaty, drained expression Ali wore at the end of the "night" recalled an image of Coltrane leaning against the wall in a cellar club in New York, also dripping in sweat, also inhaling deeply on a cigarette, also looking peaceful, anticipating the storms of passion and confusion brewing within, but with an air of well-earned temporary release.

These forms are successfully expressive. The channeling of psychic splits obviously worked; this ritual form provided catharsis and temporary resolution for its adherents. Things are culturally what they are supposed to be. The highest and deepest reach of the ecstatic twisting and writhing was expected in advance, and a meaningful interpretation for both the actors and the audience was at hand. The whole sequence was bounded, and carefully if unobtrusively supervised by the *moqaddem* lest it burst those bounds. The line between observer and participant was perfectly clear, which greatly facilitated the comprehension and enjoyment of the whole evening for me. It was all beautifully done.

Where a successful cultural form provides an on-going framework for interpreting and generating experience, here the experience of the Other is most comprehensible. Boundaries are easily discernible, symbols are neatly situated, and sequence is explicitly controlled. It is here, not surprisingly, that anthropology has been most successful in describing and understanding other cultures. Yet it is in the less explicitly shaped and less overtly significant areas of day-to-day activity and common-sense reasoning that most cultural differences are embedded. Thematic observation is disturbingly difficult, for these phenomena are everywhere, thereby proving the most opaque to the methodologies we have developed. There are no clear boundaries to conclusively limit and define cultural performance. Ritual certainly has its complexities, but they are of a different order from those more scattered, fragmentary, and partial orderings which give coherence to social life.

*   *   *

Ali and I were now steadfast companions. Despite the linguistic barriers we got along famously. We joked about how *'ayyan* my Arabic was—how enervated, feeble, and inadequate. This type of comment would invariably bring gales of laughter from Ali and Soussi. They thoroughly enjoyed these ironic twists in which one used subtle constructions or played on nuances to demonstrate how little I controlled the language. We passed many such hours together, joking, pushing, prodding, and drinking tea.

I also learned why Soussi was so profoundly unconcerned about selling anything in his shop. He had another occupation: he was a pimp. In fact, both he and Ali operated a large, if shabby, prostitution ring. They recruited Berber girls from the surrounding mountain villages and set them up in Sefrou. Prostitution was a flourishing subculture in Sefrou. Almost every Moroccan man I knew had his initiation into heterosexual activity through a visit to the prostitutes.

The girls themselves seemed to thrive (at first) on their new-found freedom, buying expensive clothes and jewelry which they had longed for in their mountain villages, and they appeared to treat their clients with familiarity and conviviality. In any case, men in Sefrou and in the countryside spoke with genuine warmth about their encounters with them. There is a sharp and clear differentiation made in Morocco between wives, who are to cook, have babies, and preserve the family honor, and women of pleasure. The prostitutes are supposedly fun-loving, and the men in Sefrou spent many hours over tea embellishing fanciful accounts of evening, days, or mornings spent with them.

Many of these girls marry after several years. Although they have lost their honor, they have distinct advantages as prospective wives (usually for a divorced man). They would, of course, have a very low bride price. They themselves were often moderately wealthy. Men said that they made good wives, because they had sown their wild oats early and be-

A young housewife in Sefrou.

come dependable later. Regardless, they were a large subculture in Sefrou, as elsewhere in Morocco. Although they definitely formed an out-group, they were not systematically despised or ostracized in the medina.

Soussi's store and Ali's shop across the road, which also doubled as his curing center, were the way stations for these girls, who eventually found their way into the mellah. As the Jews abandoned this quarter, it has been reoccupied by poor rural Berbers and a large population of prostitutes.

After a month or so of sitting around in front of Soussi's store, I was almost a co-conspirator in his comic efforts to drive away those seeking to buy clothes. I came to know Ali's girlfriend. Ali was married and had several children, but this Berber girl from Immouzer de Marmoucha, a Berber town high in the Middle Atlas mountains, was his true love (*hobb*, as he put it). She lived in his small office across from Soussi. I guessed that she had been a prostitute, or was at least intending to become one, when Cupid struck. She was always shy with me, and my '*ayyan* Arabic did not help matters; but she certainly knew who I was and came to accept me as part of the roguish circle which gravitated to Soussi's store.

One day, after the wedding dispute, Ali said that Mimouna, his true love, had to go home to visit her mother; why didn't I come along? Translated, this meant why didn't I drive them the hundred miles or so? I was delighted to agree; this vote of confidence signaled the crossing of another barrier. At the time, complicated negotiations (described below) were being conducted about my taking up residence in the village of Sidi Lahcen, and since Ali was my principal

An old Berber woman visiting Sefrou's market.

spokesman, the idea of doing him an important favor seemed like a good one. Besides, I was eager to get out of Sefrou, and Marmoucha was an area far removed from familiar terrain. Its market was famous, and I hoped to see authentic Berber crafts there. I was also curious to see how Ali was going to act with Mimouna's family. Would he pretend to be a suitor, or was his real relationship with Mimouna acknowledged? Thoughts of the romantic setting and a possible sexual encounter of my own combined to whet my appetite for the journey.

One day the next week, four of us—myself, Ali, Mimouna, and an unemployed cousin of Soussi's— squeezed ourselves into my little Simca and were off. It was a beautiful, cloudless day, and we drove joyously away from Sefrou into the mountain areas. The French had built good roads to facilitate the movement of troops and goods, but ours was the only car on the road. The Middle Atlas turns into a series of gradually ascending, rather barren plateaus which are used mainly for seasonal grazing. These plateaus are punctuated by a series of rapid ascents providing a spectacular view of the empty land below. As we approached Marmoucha, the forest cover turned to pine and began to thicken. Marmoucha itself can be spotted from far away. It is perched on a jagged set of bluffs which jut out some hundred yards from the steep mountains behind. A large waterfall emerges below. It had been a center of resistance, first to the sultans of Morocco, and later to the French. It is strategically well-placed, with a panoramic view in front and rugged mountains behind. It was finally humbled (in the mid 1930's) only through the use of bombing.

Marmoucha looks larger from a distance than it does from the inside. There is one main street on which the government buildings are found, and a large open field for the market. The market was in full swing when we arrived, but compared to Sefrou, it was quiet and the craft goods were disappointing.

After a perfunctory visit to the *qaid*, roughly sub-governor, himself a young man from a powerful family in Sefrou, who lamented the cold and how difficult the Berbers were to govern, we proceeded on to Mimouna's house. Her family lived in a simple, crude stone house on the edge of town. It was not built in the more usual urban compound style, but was a rustic two-room cabin.

Mimouna's mother greeted us like long-lost children. Clearly, she knew the score. She immediately put the kettle on to brew the strong and invigorating mountain herbal tea. We chatted a bit and she referred to me as the *moul-taxi* owner, or chief of the taxi—quite appropriately, I thought. My feeble Arabic was greeted with warm but hearty laughter, which effectively discouraged much discussion on my part. Most of the time, in any case, they spoke Berber.

After lunch, we left Marmoucha for an excursion. It was not at all evident to me where we were going, but it seemed adventurous and we were all in a marvelous mood. The two Berber girls, Mimouna and her younger sister (whom I found prettier), left by themselves and walked the five or six miles out of town, down the winding highway and then off the road to a path which led along a river bank. This seemed a bit bizarre to me. It was not obvious what appearances were being kept up, because the girls were hardly inconspicuous. The long walk took them through the main street and then down the side of the mountain, leaving them still visible from above. We, the men, drove. Who was I to question this? Once out of town, we turned and parked the car a few hundred yards off the road. If this was supposed to be camouflage, it was ludicrous; although the car could not be seen from the highway, it was clearly visible from town.

We rendezvoused with the girls and midst much giggling, smiling and romping, proceeded to follow on foot the course of the river bank as it twisted its way up the side of a steep valley. We were soon isolated; I had the feeling of being in real backwoods country. Culturally, it was also a startling experience. As we left the highway, town, and society behind, I felt a mounting excitement, as if personal inhibitions and social conventions were also being left behind.

The little mining trail came to an end and we simply followed the river. There was little chatter, but a certain amount of playing. Ali gave the Berber girls piggyback rides each time we crossed the river. They rocked him like a horse, pulled his hair, and bit his ears, which produced screams of protest from him and uproarious laughter from them. There was running and chasing and then slow climbing with mutual aid and hand-holding. Soussi's cousin, being somewhat obese and in a grouchy mood, fell farther and farther back, but the four of us proceeded on our way.

I was bewildered. I had no idea where we were going. I had never before had this kind of sensual interaction in Morocco. Although it was incredibly welcome it seemed too good to be true. Haunting

super-ego images of my anthropologist persona
thickened my consciousness as the air became purer
and the play freer. Both Ali and the Berber girls let me
be, not shunning me but not pushing either, leaving
the definition of my limits up to me. I felt wondrously
happy—it was the best single day I was to spend in
Morocco.

After an hour or so we paused. Ali pointed ahead
and seemed to be saying that our destination was
around the bend. Not realizing that we had a destination, this aroused my curiosity and gave me a twinge
of angst. You mean this is going to end?

We started up again. We were high up now, where
the air was chilly and the river moved more swiftly.
As we turned the bend before us, we came upon an
enclosed valley in which sat a small, ugly enclosure
made of concrete. It was extremely disconcerting,
having walked through such pristine country, to
come upon a building of any sort. High up on the
opposing ridge we could see some men on mules
proceeding down in our direction. We sat on the
steps of the building, catching our breath and watching their slow, spiraling descent; not saying much,
we were sitting, if not feeling, in the position of chas-
tened children. The men approached (actually they
did not get too close, because their path rose again on
the other bank as they passed us), nodded, and
trudged slowly out of our line of vision. The girls had
covered their faces when the men were passing by.
We were tired and winded. Soussi's cousin, still
grumbling, finally arrived.

I now noticed a slightly annoying smell. The building had looked at first glance like some sort of out-
house, but the absurdity of that idea drove the image

away, and when our attention was distracted by the oncoming men, I dropped the thought. There were sulphur springs inside. Hot, odorous, and health-giving, they said.

The building enclosed a small pool where the spring emerged from the mountain side. Ali and the two Berber sisters decided to go swimming. Swimming, nude, in Morocco! I had barely even seen a woman's face during the last few months, and here we were, after an absolutely splendid romp through the mountains, sitting down next to some sulphur springs, and they were going swimming.

Ali discreetly turned his back while undressing. All three were serious for a moment, as the ritual of disrobing seemed to bring back social conceptions of prudery. Even in public baths, men would undress facing the wall and shield their genitals, either by keeping their undergarments on or by covering themselves with their hands. This evoked a strong sense of *pudeur* rather than shame or guilt. Images of the baths in Sefrou rushed through my mind as I sat watching them. The wonder stemmed from my euphoria, the remoteness of the anxiety and travail of fieldwork, and the warmth and camaraderie I felt with my *compagnons de demi-monde*. The almost complete absence of linguistic communication combined with the intimacy, grace, and unambiguity of gesture to give the whole afternoon a dream-like quality, punctured only by the reemergence of my self-reflective consciousness. From time to time, it occurred to me that the sequences did not make sense, the orientations and implications were missing and we seemed to be simply carried along.

I did not go swimming myself. I was too timid. So I

sat on the edge of the pool while Ali and the Berber
sisters splashed each other. There was no strong
sexual tone to this. I am not sure why, but it was not
there. Perhaps it was friendship they felt, perhaps
the physical relaxation after the hike, perhaps a certain restraint in my presence.

They dried each other, dressed, and we were off
again back down the mountain. The trip back was
also quiet and quicker. The sun was setting, it was
chilly, and the river waters felt really cold this time.
Still feeling euphoric and comradely, we walked to
the waiting car, greeted a solitary fisherman who
gave us knowing looks, resumed our social persona,
pushed the car out of the mud, and went back to
Marmoucha.

Mimouna's mother and two other children were
waiting for us. They had a fire going and a charcoal-
scorched kettle bubbling. We smiled at each other,
and she asked *moul-taxi la-bas* (how's the driver?)
and we awaited dinner. During dinner the others
talked amongst themselves in Berber and I sat con-
tentedly savoring marvelous images of the afternoon. After tea and another set of exchanges in
Arabic, it was clearly time for bed. Ali took me into
the next room and asked me if I wanted to sleep with
one of the girls. Yes, I would go with the third
woman who had joined us for dinner. She had her
own room next door, so we could have our privacy.
Before we left the house, Ali took me aside, and
shuffling, said that he had promised to pay her but
he didn't have any money. Everyone wished
everyone a fine night, and we left.

We did not say more than a few words to each
other. My few Arabic expressions became garbled

and confused in my mind. So, silently and with an affectionate air, she indicated that I should sit on a low pillow while she made the bed. The room was a simple, rectangular one with a small attachment next to it housing a wash basin. Aside from the few pillows and charcoal burner for tea, there was only the bed. The warmth and non-verbal communication of the afternoon were fast disappearing. This woman was not impersonal, but she was not that affectionate or open either. The afternoon had left a much deeper impression on me.

This feeling was reinforced the next morning. We all had coffee together and then piled into the car. The ride back to Sefrou, down the curving empty highway, was glorious. We sang and joked all the way. Ali teased me, asking the Berber girl I had spent the night with if Monsieur Paul was *shih*, which is the opposite of *'ayyan* and means strong, energetic, full of life. *Numero wahed*, first class, she kindly replied, and then both Soussi's portly cousin and Ali demanded to know the most insistent and central of Moroccan questions: *shal*? In most cases this means "how much," but in this case it meant "how many times?"—the clearest gauge of how *shih* I was. I teasingly answered *bezzef*, many times. They were not at all satisfied with such generalities. The question was repeated to everyone's amusement several more times and received the same answer.

Finally, we saw Sefrou, a green oasis in the deforested plain, visible from many miles away. The girls put on their djellabas and veils (almost all prostitutes wear veils) and it was clear that we were almost back again.

4. Entering

Despite my by now solid relations with Ali and friends, I was becoming increasingly annoyed by my slow progress with Arabic. By the end of the summer I was truly anxiety-ridden. The prospect of moving into an environment where Arabic was the only language was intimidating. I found myself talking French a great deal. Obviously, I was not going to make substantial progress in that milieu. The balance swung toward my making concrete moves for leaving Sefrou. There were a limited number of possibilities. I wanted to work with rural Arabic speakers. Although all of the Berber tribesmen speak Arabic, it seemed that good fieldwork should be done in a group's primary language. I would save Berber for another field trip.

The town of Bhalil, a former Roman outpost perched on a craggy hill, overlooking its fields and olive trees below, was a possibility. It was rather larger and more urban that I was bargaining for, however, and its high endogamy and peculiar historical development made it appear atypical. I would keep it in reserve, as an alternate choice. Azzaba, a small Arabic-speaking village some twenty kilometers from Sefrou, with a moribund saint's cult of no particular distinction, had little to recommend it.

This left two other villages, both Arabic speaking, both with saints' tombs and holy lineages. The first was Sidi Yussef, a cluster of settlements several kilometers due south of Sefrou. It was ecologically in a rather interesting site, with a complicated irrigation system. Berber speakers and Arabic speakers lived together there, but its saint's descendants had frittered away their spiritual reputation in years of squabbling and internecine battles. Since religion was to be one of my chief areas of investigation, this was a drawback.

The other possibility, and the one to which I had been drawn even before coming to Morocco, was Sidi Lahcen Lyussi. This village has remained a traditional religious center, boasting the largest shrine in this section of the Middle Atlas Mountains. The *musem* or saint's festival was still being held and was well-attended by the tribes. There was a complex ecological setting, and sociologically the village was sufficiently diverse. Only half of the nine hundred inhabitants were members of the four saintly lineages. The rest of the village was composed of descendants of Berber groups who had come there over the years seeking sanctuary, and of the purportedly indigenous inhabitants, known locally as the "children of the slaves."

I chose Sidi Lahcen Lyussi. Making the choice was not difficult, but gaining entry posed some strategic problems. Although I never succeeded in getting all of the details, from what I have been able to piece together there was a group in the village who opposed my entry. They had two main objections, both linked to my association with Ali. First, anything Ali advocated, it turned out, was certain to generate a counterreaction of equal and opposite force. His activities in Sefrou were well known and considered

Moroccan school children are rambunctious and self-confident.

shameful. Second, the villagers moralized about this saint's descendant who was neglecting his wife, engaged with prostitutes, and tied in with the Aissawa brotherhood. In sum, Ali was quite definitely persona non grata in Sidi Lahcen. As he himself was quick to point out, there was a great deal of sheer jealousy, resentment, and backstabbing in these attacks on him, true as they might be. Indeed, I later discovered that many of the men in the village were envious of the high life which Ali seemed to be leading.

Ali was a first-rate informant. He was intelligent, quick to learn, patient, cooperative, and vivacious. But I do not think that these qualities alone explain his success as an informant. Ali, like several other people with whom I worked, was a marginal character in his own social world. He was not the average villager, he was far from the solid-citizen stereotype of Sefrou, and he had not become involved with the French. Several important consequences followed from this.

Ali was more self-reflective about his society and his place in it than most other Moroccans I knew. He had rejected village life and was paying the price for his rejection; he knew this and could explain clearly why he had chosen that path. It had not been an easy thing to do. He had been forced to work out reasons and defenses to justify and explain his action, both for himself and for his detractors. He had also pasted together his own mode of living in Sefrou. Already being ostracized by large segments of the community, he would mock the bonds of social control by flaunting his freedom. This distinguished him existentially not only from many of the lycée students

As are some old Berbers.

who were critical of village life and Sefrou's society (although their criticisms tended to remain abstract), but also from some of the men in the village, who although discontented were still quite bound by conventional constraints. In a word, Ali was more self-conscious than defensively self-justifying; he had developed practical alternatives for himself, shaky as they were.

Ali had deliberately pursued me: partly because he was curious and adventurous, partly because he saw the possibility of income, and partly because he was relatively immune to the community's social control. He had worked with other anthropologists who had come to Sefrou; he knew the ropes, and was committed to continuing the relationship. This helps to explain his rapid reestablishment of ties after our dispute. It also helps to explain the energy he put into getting me into his home village. Despite all the conflict, he knew that the more he did for me the more I was dependent on him, the more I would reciprocate, the more I became "his" anthropologist. This possessive type of relationship is quite common in Morocco. How to limit and control the tendency of informants toward possessiveness was a central problem throughout my fieldwork.

The things which made Ali a good informant also made him a liability in other contexts. This was highlighted during the disputes about my entry into Sidi Lahcen. Ali could not easily rally a faction to my cause; in the villagers' eyes there was nothing to be gained by supporting his efforts on my behalf. Although he was a member of the saintly lineages, so was his wife, consequently he had many enemies there because of his abusive disrespect of her. He exacerbated the situation by constantly baiting the villagers about their "country-bumpkin" ways, their moral hypocrisy, and their envy. It seems, therefore, that when Ali came to the village to announce that I was going to live there, a general cry of opposition greeted him. Any friend of Ali's was no friend of theirs.

But Ali had several strong cards to play. He knew that the local governor and sub-governor had approved the project, and he let the villagers know this in no uncertain terms. By so doing, it seems, he turned a generalized opposition into a fervent ambivalence. The short-lived opposition front cracked. Several villagers apparently realized that with such allies I was going to get into the village sooner or later anyway. They also realized that Ali himself was not going to move back to Sidi Lahcen, and that at least they would not have to deal with him. Here was a situation which involved risks. But where there is risk, there is also the possibility of gain.

During the tense period I spent anxiously waiting around Soussi's store, several men from the village had drifted by. They would come in, look me over, engage in a bit of perfunctory chatter, and then leave. They were sizing me up, but the standards they were using were unclear. Ali and Soussi were maintaining a good front and feeding me hollow words of encouragement while refusing to supply me with any specifics.

I am not sure what my reaction would have been had I fully understood the dynamics of the situation

at the time. No doubt, I would have become discouraged and passive at first. How could I work in a
village where they didn't want me? I'd go somewhere else. The naiveté of such a reaction is extraordinary. There would have been opposition anywhere, including Sefrou. The only real alternative
would have been to give up the project. To think that
a culture which thrives on the agonistic clash of wills,
where assertions of character and denials of those
assertions are the fabric of social life, where domination is highly valued and conflict an everyday
occurrence—to think that all of this should suddenly,
at my appearance, be transformed into a concord of
mutual respect, understanding, and open acceptance is laughable.

In fact, I was forcing my way into the village
through my official connections. That was the only
way that it could be done. Informing the officials had
been unavoidable, but their approval had made the
affair a dangerous one from the villagers' perspective. To think that these rural countrymen should
have accepted my proposal at face value and graciously granted it in the spirit of mutual respect between cultures is absurd. Why, the villagers asked,
should a rich American want to move into a poor
rural village and live by himself in a mud house when
he could be living in a villa in Sefrou? Why us? Why
get ourselves into a situation where the government
holds us jointly responsible for this stranger? What's
in it for us? The risks are all too evident.

What could I have possibly answered? The further-
ing of anthropology? My career? Broadening their

horizons? A small amount of money for a few villagers? Their perceptions were accurate enough. In their
terms, there really was no reason to allow me into the
village.

Yet I had come to Morocco to live in a village. The
only justification I briefly entertained, the bad faith of
which is all too apparent, was that I could offer the
community something. I could not increase their agricultural production. I could not cure their diseases
or get them work. I could not make the rains come on
time. Perhaps I could teach them English. When I
finally did arrive in the village, I suggested this rather
timidly. There was a polite but tepid response which
was soon passed over by all concerned.

There may be situations in which the anthropologist can directly aid the community, but my guess is
that they are rare. I have heard "aid" advocated most
fervently by those who have never done fieldwork.
The position seems more justifiable within one's own
society, where thought, action, and responsibility
are more closely connected. Having thought about
the problem over the years, however, it is unclear to
me what I could have done to aid the villagers which
would not have been the kind of blatant interference
in their affairs for which we criticize A.I.D. programs. If the ethical status of the anthropologist is
ambiguous, then the do-gooder, whatever his cause,
would seem to be even more profoundly disqual-
ified.

The advocacy of political activity as a role for the
anthropologist also seems highly untenable in this
kind of situation. I was the only foreigner living in
the entire jurisdictional circle of the gendarmerie. All

of my activities were observed, reported, and dis-
torted by various factions, as we shall see. If I had
been organizing or advocating anti-government action it would have gotten back to local government
bureaus with lightning speed. There is no question
that I would have been forced to leave the country,
and a distinct possibility of being thrown into jail.
This might sound like an attractive adventure in Paris
or Berkeley, but in Morocco it seemed frighteningly
nonsensical.

Once one accepts a definition of anthropology as
consisting of participant observation, as I had, then
one's course of action is really governed by these
oxymoronic terms; the tension between them defines
the space of anthropology. Observation, however, is
the governing term in the pair, since it situates the
anthropologists' activities. However much one
moves in the direction of participation, it is always
the case that one is still both an outsider and an observer. That one is an outsider is incessently apparent. The cloud of official approval always hung over
me, despite my attempts to ignore it. My gestures
were wrong, my language was off, my questions
were strange, and interpersonal malaise was all too
frequently the dominant mood, even after many
months when some of the grossest differences had
been bridged by repetition and habit. No matter how
far "participation" may push the anthropologist in
the direction of Not-Otherness, the context is still
ultimately dictated by "observation" and externality.
In the dialectic between the poles of observation and
participation, participation changes the anthropologist and leads him to new observation, whereupon

new observation changes how he participates. But this dialectical spiral is governed in its motion by the starting point, which is observation.

*   *   *

Finally word came from the village: I could move in. The leaders of the saintly lineages had changed their minds. I was welcome in Sidi Lahcen, and would be under their protection. I could rent a small one-room construction which had been used as a storehouse for corn.

The next week was joyously spent in making preparations, buying provisions, and feeling relieved. So what if my Arabic was weak and I was entering a hostile situation; the "real" fieldwork was finally underway. Despite all the difficulties which lay ahead, without my knowing it, the worst was over. From this point on, movement was both discernible and consoling. I packed a bed, some cushions, a low table, and a simple desk into a borrowed station wagon one fine morning and was off, too happy to be anxious.

As one drives out of Sefrou, the contrasts at first are marked. After passing the new barracks-like extensions of the city and a lycée, one enters an open plateau. One side of the French-built two-lane highway is covered with scrub and rocks. This was grazing land, but with significant decline in seasonal grazing and sheepherding; the black tents of the Ait Yussi tribesmen are only seldom seen this close to Sefrou. On the other side of the highway, several kilometers further south, lies a series of mechanized farms reminiscent of the Sais. They formed one of the original areas of colonization in the region. The land which had been collectively owned was bought from the tribes in a complicated transaction involving the major banks and a group of industrious small farmers, through the intermediary offices of the Protectorate government. The tribes traded this arid grazing land for richer plots many miles away. Dams were built, fields cleared, trees planted, silos erected, and machines brought in. The boundaries of this modernized area are visually striking; the scrub and deforested hills begin again immediately at its perimeter.

Past the next set of hills, on yet another plateau, one can see several cactus-ringed settlements spread over the rolling countryside. The land now seems more fertile. Government work teams are clearing it of rock and constructing long, irregular, red-brown stone hedges. At the end of this stretch of cultivated terrain is the village of Azzaba, which serves as a minor market and government post. Despite its school, and its government-sponsored butcher shops and irrigation facilities, Azzaba remains dusty and distinctly undynamic. People say that the water is bad, that it is hot, and that the saint who is buried there and whose name has been forgotten has no *baraka*. The village does sit right in the middle of an exposed area slightly raised above the plateau, and the water there does have a distinctly unpleasant taste.

After Azzaba one is really into the foothills of the Middle Atlas. The inclines are steeper, the road curves much more sharply, and villages are found only where there is water. Between them lie long, deforested plateaus showing only scrub and an occasional tree. The herds are largely gone, and it is quiet.

One leaves the paved highway several kilometers out of Azzaba and turns onto a poorly graded, gravel-covered road which crosses one of these desolate stretches. After a steep climb one achieves another vast panorama. The car eases up as the land levels out and one can cruise across this plane on the lookout for life. Here and there off to the side one sees Berber compounds perched on slight elevations. These compounds are built like fortresses, and indeed they were used as such during the periods of tribal dissidence which have marked Moroccan history. A Berber proverb asserts that Berbers live alone like real men, while Arabs live clustered together in fear, like sheep. The rural Arabic speakers reply that Berbers fight with everyone like wild animals, whereas Arabs are men, who prefer to live in each other's company.

One can see from some distance away that the road reaches a hilltop and disappears from view. After a short descent, following a hairpin turn, the rush of green that greets one is startling. Sidi Lahcen Lyussi is located on a fault line in the mountains which runs up a long valley. Water is plentiful and a crude set of canals defines the village's agricultural area. According to legend, when the saint left Azzaba he continued on until he reached this break in the mountains, tasted the sweet water, and proclaimed that it was here that he would settle. Be that as it may, there are over ten thousand olive trees nestled in and up the sides of the valley and surrounding slopes.

Two large whitewashed buildings dominate the village-scape: a large mosque, and adjacent to it, a truly distinctive green-tiled saint's tomb. In front of these two structures is a flat area of beaten earth around whose perimeters are clustered houses and stores. This open area is both the center of the village and the area on which the *musem* or saint's festival is held each year in the fall and spring.

The whole of Sidi Lahcen is really composed of four clusters. Farther up the valley, extending several kilometers, are the three other settlements. The smallest of these, two kilometers up the valley and perched high on a crest, consists of only a few compounds. A slightly larger one lies below it. The third settlement, larger still, is on a small plateau which overlooks the mosque, tomb, and main settlement from a distance of two hundred yards. According to legend, each of these settlements was originally the home of one of Sidi Lahcen's sons. Today each is more or less the center of a lineage, but the correlations are far from exact. In any case, almost all of the non-descendants of the saint live in the largest of these clusters. The area around the tomb is considered to be a religious sanctuary, and during troubled periods Berber families could seek refuge there.

As one slowly descends the S-shaped curve which leads to the *musem* area and tries to avoid the scrawny dogs, chickens, and children who dart in front of the car, the village looks much shabbier than it does from above. The houses which line the road are of mud and stone, seemingly slapped together in a haphazard fashion, and from the outside at least, they certainly seem in need of repair. Here and there one can spot more substantial looking compounds built of cement, but they are clearly the exception in this village. The road is rutted and at times runs dangerously close to the edge.

The first impression the villagers give is also one of poverty. Their djellabas are bedraggled and mud-spattered, and many have no shoes on. Groups of men are seated in the dirt in front of the three stores which lie below the road and form a back-stop for the *musem* space. Seemingly engaged in conversation and involved in making crude baskets out of the tough scrub which lines the arid plateaus above, there was little movement of acknowledgement from these men as we pulled up. The car was greeted, however, by what seemed like hundreds of *drari*— which is inadequately translated as children. These fearless little monsters surrounded the car, much to the annoyance of their elders. Screaming, yelling, and pushing they proceeded to examine all of my possessions. One of the villagers' main fears, it turns out, was that these drari would do some irreparable damage either to me or my belongings. Their fathers threatened them with beatings, curses, and exclamations, to little or no avail. My new residence was still filled with corn, so we had to wait in the midst of the *drari* and their nervous elders while it was hurriedly cleaned. Finally we got the few pieces of furniture into the house and a council of elders decided that the *drari*, now climbing over each others' backs to peer through the windows, had to be brought under control. What sticks and stones could not ac-complish, moral coercion could: upon being told that they would be reported to their teachers, the *drari* disappeared in a twinkling, as if by magic. The anthropologist made a mental note.

Ali delivered the sheep, which he had suggested I bring as a gift, to the saint's tomb. He had never specified who this gift was for, and as I discovered later, how to share the slaughtered sheep was a source of conflict. Ali apparently made off with the hide.

The next two days were like a dream. I arranged my belongings in the house. I said "everything is all right, today is Tuesday, yesterday was Monday, it is hot, supper is good, yes, really good" and "yes, I like Morocco" and any Arabic phrase I could muster up as many times as I could bear it; I drank many cups of mint tea, walked around doing initial exploring of the village, and sat in the store where the men played cards.

The food during the first few days was truly delicious. I was invited to eat with the richest man in the village, a veteran of the Indo-China campaign and an ex-chauffeur of the Crown Prince, who had suddenly lost his vision from the effects of an old wound and therefore received a substantial pension from the French. He publicly displayed his hospitality to me and let it be known that I was under his protection. The fresh olive oil in which everything was prepared, the bread straight from the oven, the large quantities of newly slaughtered meat, the hot peppers, the strong coffee and sweet tea, all served in his compound overlooking the village and fields below, was terribly romantic.

On the fourth day a gendarme wearing tinted glasses arrived with a man from one of the other clusters in Sidi Lahcen. The gendarmes in Morocco, following the French system, form an elite police force with jurisdiction outside the cities. In my experience, the gendarmes are intelligent, well-trained, efficient, and generally disliked.

The gendarme came to my house and knocked at the door. The village was crowded with Berbers, who came to Sidi Lahcen every Friday for a communal prayer at the large mosque. They provided an attentive audience. The gendarme refused my Arabic greetings, answering in what can only be described as impeccable French. He asked if I had my *permit de sejour* and could he see it? I said certainly, and handed it to him as well as my driver's license. We went out to the car, which was now parked some distance from my house, next to the compound of the rich veteran who had been offering me hospitality; it was felt that the *drari* would not dare roll it down the hill if it were under the protection of such a powerful man. In full view of a large audience, we talked briefly. I was somewhat defensive and cold, saying that I had registered the car with the police in Sefrou. The car was fine, he said, thank you for your trouble; but since I was now in the countryside I must also register with the gendarmerie. There was no problem, though. They knew all about me. In fact I would be the first person to register with them that year. This was all a simple formality, merci bien, one of these days. . . .

The gendarme and I had been speaking in low tones and in French. It turns out that while our conversation was progressing, on the road above us a

man from another faction was giving a running interpretation of what was occurring, a version that
seemed to confirm all the apprehensions which pre-
ceded my entry. As far as I could reconstruct it later,
he was telling the crowd that the gendarmes were
furious because a *nazrani*, a Christian, was living in a
saint's village. The gendarme already had a list of all
the people who had so much as greeted me and they
would probably be thrown in jail. Therefore no one
should even talk to me.

This had the desired effect. By the time I returned
to my house I knew that something drastic had happened. Shortly thereafter a delegation appeared, led
by several men with whom I had begun working and
the official village representative on the regional
council. They told me that because the government
was angry, they could not work with me. Further,
could they have the notes I had been making. They
were sorry but the government was strong and powerful, and there was nothing they could do about it.

Shocked, I put up my stoutest front, maintaining
that the gendarme had said nothing of the sort. I did
have permission to be there and the government certainly knew about me. We should go to the *qaid* tomorrow and he would back me up. In good Moroccan rhetorical style I had countered a strong gambit
with an equally strong counterattack. They were unsure. They agreed that the *moumtil*, their representative, would go with me to Sefrou and we would see
the *qaid*. Until then no one would talk to me.

There was no food that night except a can of sar-
dines I had brought and some instant coffee. I spent

the night listening to the "Pop Club" from Paris. It was such a totally overwhelming experience that I did not even feel consciously upset. It was also one of those lucid moments when the different stakes involved were revealed. I had no idea what the gendarme had said to the villagers. If there was any truth at all to the rumor (and I couldn't see how there could be), then of course the villagers were correct in backing off. Something very strange was going on. Perhaps it was the residual effect of the debate about my entry into the village. If so, then a counterattack on my part was necessary. Factionalism being what it is in Morocco, where there are enemies there are also potential allies. I had to discredit the rumor and its source or I was finished in Sidi Lahcen.

Early the next morning we drove into Sefrou. The *qaid* ushered us in rather ceremoniously. I told him in French that it seemed that one of his gendarmes had come to the village and told the villagers not to talk to me. I was confused about the reasons for this and the villagers were upset. Would he be so kind as to talk to the *moumtil* and explain to him what was going on? After questioning the *moumtil*, the *qaid*, with a somewhat puzzled expression, picked up the phone and called in the gendarme. He entered, greeted us, and listened. When he heard the story, he looked hurt, his pride wounded. He had said no such thing. He had come only to check my registration, exactly as he had told me. The rest was none of his doing. The *qaid* thanked him and he left.

The *qaid*, a soft-spoken and even-tempered man—one of the reasons, I might add, that he was

neither respected nor feared—explained clearly that
everything was in order. The government had given
me permission, it was all right to work with me,
whoever made up the story would be dealt with se-
verely. The *moumtil* seemed convinced. The *qaid*
asked me a few polite questions about Ibn Khaldun's
philosophy of history, which I answered, and we
left. On the way back I realized how drained I was.
Round one was a success, but there were obviously
more to come. Now that the government's backing
was clear, I intended to find out what had happened.

The man who had been giving the running com-
mentary was a leader of a faction in one of the upper
clusters. He seems to have decided that I was a potentially valuable resource, and that either I would
work with him and be under his influence or I would
not work there at all. His scenario anticipated that his
tactics would scare everyone else away, so he could
make me a generous offer of lodging and hospitality
in his settlement. Several months later, he did make
me such an offer. By then, I was firmly and produc-
tively ensconced in a web of relationships which I
had no desire to break. I would have been happy to
add him as an informant. Preliminary negotiations
and tea-drinking visits began. But they were quickly
sabotaged by the men with whom I was now working. I belonged to them, and they were not going to
permit someone else to horn in.

My initial entry accomplished, I was now faced
with the task of conveying who I was and what I was
going to do in the village. My purpose in being there

remained unclear to most of the villagers, even to those with whom I spent many, many hours. I told the villagers that I was a *taleb*, a student of history and the science of society—which are both classical Arabic concepts, presenting no translation problems. I said that my university had sent me to do a study of the history of the village and then report back to them. I would probably write a book. I had several examples ready to offer as evidence, and then, God willing, I too would become a professor at a university. This much was understandable and acceptable to the villagers. The term *taleb*, however, carries a religious connotation in Arabic, and since I wasn't a Muslim, this created some confusion.

Despite the myriad divisions which fragment Moroccan social life, there is one cultural conviction on which I never found either hesitation or disagreement: the world is divided into Muslims and non-Muslims. Islam does provide a mediating category for the "peoples of the book," Christians and Jews. They, too, have received a divine revelation, but it is incomplete. Mohammed is sovereign among the prophets, for his revelation combines those of the Jews and the Christians and completes them. These people have the right under Islam to practice their own religion so long as they acknowledge their inferior role by paying special taxes and by accepting a variety of symbolic and material burdens. That this can be a relatively workable, if onerous, arrangement is attested to by Muslim-Jewish relations in Morocco for the last thousand years.

It is workable, however, only as long as Muslim dominance is clear. My religion did not interest them at all. They never questioned me on my assertion that I was a Christian. After all, they had the truth. A pervasive malaise, however, was symbolized by the widespread fear that I was a missionary. This persisted throughout my stay, even to the very last day. By then it should have been clear that I had not interfered with, denigrated, or tried to alter anyone's religious beliefs. Yet, cries of *messihi*, missionary, still rang out from a group of *drari*. Although it was annoying, such a tenacious identification was significant.

There was a dormant fear of Christianity. The villagers knew that the Christian lands were now more powerful than the Islamic countries. This led to a lingering anxiety that this political and military power would be converted into an attempt at religious dominance, which was, after all, the most important sphere of life in villagers' eyes.

This seemed to be the only possible reason why a rich young American (me) would leave the comforts of home in order to live with them. I must be after something crucially important. The subversion of their religion was one of the few things they could imagine to be worthy of such a sacrifice. That I did not try to interfere in religious matters, I now understand, was irrelevant. The constant expression of pure and noble intentions is a rhetorical art which Moroccans have raised to the level of cultural performance, and they never take such professions of purity at face value. I did my best to assuage these fears during my stay. I stressed time and again that my interests were historical and social, but I doubt that I was very convincing. Still, a modus vivendi was worked out. Their anxieties were never totally absent, but I managed, for the most part, to keep them at bay.

*   *   *

The problem of finding, cultivating, and changing informants in a small village is one of the most delicate facing the anthropologist. There are no neutral roles for him. He may become involved in politics and social divisions even before he enters the village. In my case, from the very beginning I was associated politically with the descendants of the village saint. As they were the dominant group in the village, and since their role was crucial to my study, I was more than happy to accept such an association, at least initially. It was soon apparent, however, that they themselves were far from unified.

As we have seen, the four clusters which comprise Sidi Lahcen were loosely correlated with four lineages who traced their ancestry back to the sons of the saint. This was largely a genealogical fiction (as anthropologists call it) and not the true locus of group activity in the village. Thus, for example, in the main cluster where I was living, most of the saint's descendants belonged to one lineage (traced their descent back to one son). Socially, however, they were divided into three major sub-lineages. Each of these sub-lineages, with perhaps seventy-five to a hundred people, had as its apical ancestor one of three brothers who lived at the turn of the century. They were all saint's descendants, they were all lineage mates, and they shared a loose kinship affiliation. Beyond that, they had sharp social divergences. One of these sub-lineages, the one to which Ali belonged, was famous for its constant bickering, the refusal of its members to live in the same part of the village, and their general inability to cooperate economically, socially, or personally. The second group was highly endogamous, and lived clustered together in a set of connected compounds; its members shared a certain amount of their economic resources, and sustained whatever religious prestige the village had maintained. The third was somewhere in between, on all counts. There was much rivalry and competition between the various groups and between particular individuals. So, from the vantage point of one living in Sefrou, the descendants of the saint were an entity, whereas in Sidi Lahcen this was far from the case. Only very rarely and on specific occasions did they display any solidarity.

The first few men with whom I worked, or attempted to work, were from Ali's dissension-torn sub-lineage. There was Ali himself. There was the Sergeant Larawi, as he was called, the wealthy veteran of the French army who had offered me hospitality during the first few days. Although he was an important figure, being the wealthiest man in the village, it was obvious that I was not going to be able to do systematic work with him. He was always busy, engaged in the expansion of his agricultural holdings, and like other "big men" in Morocco he liked to ask the questions, not answer them. He was an ally to have, but there seemed to be no point in even broaching the subject of work with him. I was at his beck and call, not the other way round. He frequently came to my house at night and told stories or listened to the radio. Many of my insights into Moroccan life stem from the hours I spent with him, which complemented the more structured work I did with my informants. Not dominating the terms of the interaction also had its advantages; not being in control enriched the fieldwork.

My landlord was also from Ali's sub-lineage. Not only was he one of Ali's chief detractors, he also was engaged in a long-standing dispute with the Sergeant. He was a pious and grouchy old man, and we never had any sustained interaction. His son, however, was just the opposite—warm, gracious, and friendly. His company was always relaxing and rewarding. He was studying at the Karawiyin University in Fez, concentrating on Arabic language courses. Fortunately, he knew almost no French. He politely but firmly refused to do any regular work with me from the very beginning of my stay. This was a keen disappointment, because he was a truly promising informant. Although he had one foot out of the village and clearly wanted another life for himself, he was still loyal and respectful to his family, which was one of the most traditional in the village.

My first informant in Sidi Lahcen was also a cousin of Ali's. Mekki was a twenty-year-old part-time shepherd and storetender. Although it was immediately apparent that he lacked intelligence, this did not seem too important at first. He had spare time, he seemed eager to do the work, and in the beginning there seemed to be so many elementary and non-conceptual tasks to be done that it seemed almost anyone would suffice. But this

proved not to be the case. One of the essential qualities of a good informant is the ability to explain even
the simplest and (to him) most obvious things in a
variety of ways. The most consistently productive of
my informants displayed this quality from the start.
It was not merely patience (although that was certainly a capital virtue), or even intelligence (which
certainly helped), but rather an imaginative ability
to objectify one's own culture for a foreigner, so as
to present it in a number of ways. Mekki was almost
totally incapable of this. This was no character de-
fect on his part, but it posed an immediate dilemma.
I had to end this relationship as gracefully as possible because it was leading nowhere.

Fortunately for me, this potentially awkward
situation was avoided through a bit of luck. Mekki
heard of the possibility of some sheepherding work
with a group higher up in the mountains and decided to go off and try his luck there. I was told later
that although the villagers were fond of Mekki, they
also considered him to be a dullard. I imagine that
the men sitting around the store found it quite
amusing that the new anthropologist was working
with the village idiot.

The next young man who crossed my path was
quite a different story. He was the son of a relatively
prosperous storekeeper, who was the leader of the
loosely affiliated opposition forces in the village.
These forces, which did not really form a coherent
group, were comprised of men from a series of unre-
lated families in the village. The one large grouping
of non-saint's descendants, called the "sons of the
slaves," were tied together by only the slimmest of

genealogical fictions. Most of their connections were forgotten, and they were neither endogamous nor culturally unified. The storekeeper himself was not from this group. His own father had settled some forty years earlier in Sidi Lahcen after marauding tribes had burned their village to the ground. He had bought land which he had left to his son, who managed it well, so that he was now quite well-off by village standards. The father deeply resented the saint's descendants and had tried to build himself a power base by attacking them as being pretentious, overbearing, and hypocritical. Although this struck a chord in the region, he had not been able to transmute it into any significant political success. But he kept trying.

His son, Rashid, was incredibly quick, intelligent, sensitive, and overflowing with gossip and slander about almost everyone in the village. He came to my house after a week or so and proposed that we go for a walk together. He had heard about my attempts to get Mekki to draw a map of the village, and said he would help me with it.

That night, as we were sitting around cooking dinner, another cousin of Ali's with whom I was beginning to work told me cryptically but emphatically that I should have nothing to do with Rashid: he was a wild animal and dangerous. He refused to elaborate. It seemed to be simple jealousy or perhaps a political attempt to keep me within the saintly sub-lineages. I said that I had to work with other people, but of course I would heed his warnings. The man accepted this with a sullen air, saying again that he had warned me.

Rashid and I left early in the morning the next day. We headed for a field perhaps a mile from the village, where his father's sharecropper was plowing. The quick pace was exhilarating and the solicitiousness, which stopped just short of outright flattery, was also a pleasant change. He listened to my already improving Arabic, rephrased things for me, and most exciting of all, made suggestions as to whole areas we could jointly explore. The more elaborate and grandiose the imaginary plans, the more animated Rashid became; my spirits soared. We would first do a map, then the irrigation system, field ownership, kinship, politics, and the rest. He clearly was winning my confidence and this spurred him on. He went into the litany which potential informants, without exception, recited for me: Everyone else in the village is a liar and will deceive you, and I am the only one who will tell you the truth; they will slander me, but you are really lucky to have found me because I will save you from those scoundrels and wild animals, who will only try to steal your money.

A magnificent walk around the outlying fields filled a major part of the day. The terrain alternates between deserted, rocky stretches and intensely cultivated irrigated plots. Where there is water available, olive, fig, pomegranate, and almond trees abound. Wheat, barley, corn, and a variety of truck garden vegetables also flourish in appropriate seasons. In contrast, a few yards away, the brush and rocks bear witness to the importance of water. The rapidity of change from field to field, from hillside to hillside, provides an intensity of visual experience

which parallels the emotional intensity of the
Moroccans themselves. There is little regularity to
the land in the mountains. One side of a hill will
have good drainage and the other side poor drainage. One slope will be within the perimeter of an
irrigation system and therefore green, while an adjoining field may be fallow. From the ground, there
are no unbroken vistas of any appreciable distance.
Land holdings are fragmented and farmers maintain small plots in different parts of the valley. They
hedge their bets against the unpredictable weather
by planting different crops on different fields. Thus
in any particular sector of the valley, adjacent fields
will have a contrasting appearance.

Rashid guided me in and over, through and
around fields and hills, embellishing his sure and
casual knowledge with the local lore attached to
each field. He spoke in simple, clear Arabic, unhur-
ried and lucid. Throughout that day, Rashid wore a
mischievious grin. This slightly mocking expression
bubbled over with self-enjoyment and disdain for
the opinions of others. He had great self-confidence
and seemed to be guarding a secret which caused
him great mirth. Several times he reminded me that
people were going to slander him when I returned.

Again, he was completely correct. We continued
to work together for several weeks, drawing maps,
touring the fields, and so on, but there was a steadily mounting offensive against him. The moral attacks on his character never impressed me very
much. It was said that he had left school, fought
with his father, was a troublemaker and a rascal,
perhaps a petty thief, and in general a bad influence. In retrospect, all of these charges and several

more turned out to be basically true. But for some of the same reasons he was an excellent informant. He was on the fringe of community control; his father had to call in the gendarmes to rough him up on one occasion. He would say things and talk about people in a manner which the anthropologist cherished, strikingly direct. He was more than happy to tell me almost anything I wanted to know.

Parading around with me in front of the more respectable members of the community, knowing full well that he was provoking them, only heightened his pleasure. Rashid was the polar opposite of Mekki, my first informant. Late adolescence is a difficult time in Morocco, and Mekki bitterly anticipated the years he would have to wait before he would be married. His family was very poor and could not afford the bride price. But while Mekki sulked and saw only the difficulties and trials ahead, Rashid clung to the joys and adventures of youth, maintaining the spirited rebelliousness of the *drari*. There was little the villagers could do to control him. He had almost no work to do except errands for his father. Since he hung around the store where the men played cards, he knew most of the village gossip. He reveled in the notoriety of working with the anthropologist. He himself had nothing to lose.

Unfortunately, the political assault against him proved decisive. The saint's descendants had been seething when I began to work with Rashid because of his father's activities. It took me awhile to realize this, because they were extremely reluctant to talk about their animosities. Their hesitancy to talk about the political divisions only added fuel to their moralistic vituperation. Once I realized the depth of their feelings, I became more circumspect and cautious with Rashid.

The decisive blow came from Rashid's father, who wanted to work with me himself. That is to say, he wanted me in his camp. He was also afraid that Rashid might reveal too many embarrassing details, so he joined his enemies in arguing that Rashid was only a child and not really the right person for this important task. The choice was boiling down to Rashid or everyone else. Several days later Rashid was lured to southern Morocco by some shady scheme or other, and he was gone for many months. That solved that.

5. Respectable Information

The man who eventually became my main informant and closest associate during my stay in Sidi Lahcen was Abd al-Malik ben Lahcen. When we met, he still considered himself a young man, giving his age as either thirty or thirty-two. Since his father had died several years earlier, Malik was head of the household. He had two younger brothers, still unmarried, and his mother to look after. One brother was working at a government agricultural station in the vicinity and earning his keep. The youngest brother did the farming and took care of the animals.

Malik was the brains in the family. He did the head work and the others did the manual work. To him this was an eminently fair arrangement, since he had convinced himself and his brothers of his high intelligence. Protecting the family interests required brain-work. For example, there was a rapacious uncle who was perpetually hatching schemes to steal their land. There were many other tasks, he told me, but they remained unspecified. Despite all this supposedly time-consuming work, he had ample opportunity to work with the anthropologist.

Malik had displayed his intellectual gifts at an early age. He had done well in the local Koranic school and had continued working on memorizing the Koran even after he finished school. He also assumed an air of self-importance and learnedness. One has the impression that perhaps a century earlier this pose might have had more substantial rewards. In his teens, he hung around the village doing some farming—he developed a distinct dislike for manual labor during those years—while continuing to study at the mosque. When he was about twenty he moved to one of the neighboring Berber settlements to take a position as a *fqi* or religious teacher. His duties amounted to teaching the Koran to *drari* and calling the prayers. About six months later he moved on to a slightly more prestigious position in a larger village, but he did not last very long there either. Malik was enamored with the idea of himself as a *fqi*, a man engaged in spiritual pursuits, but the realities of the job were of another order; the endless and boring repetition of the Koran to a room full of recalcitrant *drari*, the extremely low and sporadic pay (the *fqi* lived basically on the charity of the community), and the necessity of arising in the dawn hours to call the first prayer were not at all to his liking. He abandoned his career after a year but is still known in the village, half affectionately, half mockingly, as the *fqi*.

While his father was still alive, he returned to the village, resumed some limited agricultural chores, and spent a great deal of time at the mosque, thus qualifying himself as a *taleb*, a term which designates those villagers who regularly come to the mosque to chant the Koran.

Malik was a nervous and somewhat sickly man. One of the reasons he gave for leaving his post as *fqi* was that he frequently suffered from nosebleeds which left him weak and enervated. I took him to a

French doctor after one of these nosebleeding incidents; the doctor said that he was slightly anemic but
otherwise there seemed to be nothing physically
wrong with him. Fragility, weakness, and delicacy of
constitution are looked down upon in Moroccan culture, and so Malik put up a bold front.

He was frequently worried about illness and dying. Several of his children, including his only and
much beloved son, had died, leaving him with a
deep emotional scar. His stance as a man of the spirit
combined with a great capacity for self-pity and a
weak constitution to produce a touchy and defensive
character. Malik is normally sullen, wearing a worried and anxious look, and his joking and
camaraderie often seem forced. Yet he is intelligent,
patient, and determined.

His deep determination to avoid manual labor was
one of his main reasons for seeking me out. I realized
later that Malik had come to Sefrou several times to
observe me in Soussi's store before he committed
himself. There are precious few sources of income in
the village aside from the fields, and he was obliged
to exploit any that came along, such as writing a letter
for a Berber tribesman or officiating at a circumcision
ceremony. The possibility of working with me was
thus something he seriously had to consider. After
all, it was "head" work, a consistent source of
money, and offered a mixture of prestige and notoriety. Although we never discussed it, I suspect the
fact that I was not a Muslim caused him considerable
anxiety and hesitation about engaging in a relationship with me. I do not think that he was originally a
strong supporter of my entry into the village, but

when my "formal" acceptance seemed imminent, he made his move. He came into Sefrou looking for me. I was out of the city that day, so he stayed overnight and sought me out the next morning at Soussi's store. He sat sulkily staring into space for some time before speaking. Then he announced abruptly that he would work with me, adding that he was very intelligent, honest, not greedy, and thoroughly trustworthy, and that I was privileged to have this opportunity. At this point it was still not clear to me whether I would get into the village, so I thanked him and said I would think about it. He left.

I did not see him again until I arrived in Sidi Lahcen. He helped me unpack my things but kept his distance as long as Ali was around. Only after two days did he arrive to say that he was ready to start working immediately. We would draw up a contract in French and Arabic and both keep a copy. The rate would be five *dirhems* (roughly one dollar or a day's wages on a farm) a session, and the sessions could vary in time. It would be best for both of us if we made the contract for a month. That way, if either of us wanted to back out of the agreement there would be nothing between us and everything would be just as before. If we agreed to continue, we would write another contract. This speech was presented in a formal tone. Malik had his best clothes on for the occasion. Although I could not follow exactly what he was saying, I understood the drift of it. Of course I agreed, and we proceeded to draw up the contract.

We started to work on kinship that afternoon. Patiently, speaking slowly and clearly, he made sure that I was following. He estimated how long it would take to finish the genealogies and said that he would

begin the necessary political dealings, *siyasa*, with
other lineages; he wanted everything to be correct
with my important work.

During the incident with the gendarme who had
come to register my car, Malik was petrified. He
asked me to burn the notes we had made. I gave
them to him and told him to hold on to them until
this nonsense passed. He agreed, adding that he
would not be able to work with me until everything
was straightened out. When we returned from our
visit to the *qaid*'s office, Malik eagerly and seriously
grilled the representative on all the details of the conversation. When he seemed satisfied, he turned to
me and announced that we could begin work again
that afternoon.

Although there were minor disputes and troubles
during the months which followed, Malik was the
most diligent and orderly person with whom I
worked. He became my chief informant in Sidi
Lahcen, and we covered all the essential ethnographic ground together in many, many hours of work.
Much of my basic understanding of kinship, irrigation, landowning, social structure, and formal aspects of religion stemmed from these months of
work. Malik lacked the flair of other Moroccans, but
his ploddingly persistent and highly regular work
habits more than compensated. His social position as
a solidly entrenched and respected villager certainly
helped to legitimate my presence in the village. The
Sergeant also approved of my working with Malik.
They had had a series of contractual relations in the
past which had been followed through without conflict. He publicly sanctioned my working with Malik.
With his backing, I was now secure. The proof that I

was being accepted was that people were beginning to make demands on me.

The first testing arena was my car. I hate cars. I had never owned one in America, and did not even have a license before I came to Morocco. I bought the car there because it seemed necessary. It would give me a means to explore possible fieldwork locations, and would also serve as a psychological escape hatch; the prospect of living in an isolated mountain village made me somewhat apprehensive, and I thought the car might prove essential if I got sick or needed to leave in a hurry. This was faulty reasoning, because if I broke a leg or got appendicitis I would not be able to drive anyway. The car did offer me some hours of pleasure: driving though the Middle Atlas Mountains on empty highways, singing to myself, was a great release. But once I was actually installed in the village, the car proved to be more of an annoyance than a convenience. My claustrophobia dissipated after I had been there several weeks, and the psychological rationale for the car faded.

When the demands for rides to Sefrou began, I had Malik announce that I would go to Sefrou once a week, and would take four people with me on a first-come, first-served basis. I added to Malik that if there was an emergency I would be willing to take people to the hospital. He nodded sagely and agreed that he would tell the others. What folly. I was constantly deluged with requests.

*   *   *

My first months in the village were heady stuff. I was collecting data almost as fast as I could record it. The

outline of village social and political structure seemed
to be emerging effortlessly from the material itself.
Patterns of land holdings and genealogies seemed to
be jumping off the pages. I felt little need to dally in
interpretation, and plunged ahead. It was absorbing
work, free from anxiety because the tasks were defined and progress was measurable. Malik worked
diligently and consistently. Since I was now clearly
his, he arranged for a series of other villagers to work
with me on specific topics.

Malik and I began our work with the genealogies,
because it was work that could be started with a minimal vocabulary. The formulas, "so and so, father of
so and so, married to so and so," carried us through
many hours. Here was a schematic and systematic
way to become acquainted with village groups and
their formal interrelations. At first, Malik was extremely serious and *fqi*-like. He would announce
"We are now going to work," chase out anyone who
happened to be in the room, and sit down stiffly next
to my table. We proceeded in strict order from group
to group. Later he began to loosen up. He would
throw in personal comments, usually highly sarcas-
tic ones, about the individuals involved. As trust
began to develop, he would also provide a series of
jocular commentaries about the women: this one had
huge hips, that one was a terror. This work, and
more specifically the listing of land holdings and
olive tree owners, was fairly mechanical. I could
measure my progress in the growing stacks of sheets
ripped off the clipboard to be typed the next working. This provided immediate satisfaction: my day
was finally filled with my own work, an orientation

The anthropologist toasts members of the holy lineage.

to specifics began to emerge, and I could see which particular questions remained to be answered the next day.

Another popular topic of village conversation was my departure. A constant refrain was that I would forget them, and not write. This led immediately into a discussion of who would get my furniture. It was all so open and business-like that after my first sense of affront I rather enjoyed it. They were certainly under no illusions about the transitoriness of my situation. This direct and materialistic level of exchange was a strong indication that I was being accepted. Material motives are never in disrepute in Morocco. It is only when they are absent that suspicion is aroused.

Malik and I were developing a smooth rapport. We had already renegotiated the original contract— again at his instigation—and now were formally working half a day together. Our relationship was still more a contractual one than a friendship, how- ever. The free and easy, relatively undefined type of interaction I had with Ali was absent. This was a more serious affair, and Malik himself was directing the situation. We spent time making plans for the next day, rechecking various points, talking about how to proceed, estimating the time needed to cover various topics. Our joking was guarded, not the more explosive and personalistic humor of "sound- ing" and mutual denigration at which Moroccans ex- cel. I was not invited to eat at Malik's house for quite a while, and during my whole stay I ate with him there only three times.

This was fine with me. I was absorbed and more than pleased with the work Malik was doing, both directly with the information we collected, and indirectly with the way he handled other villagers, keeping most of them somewhat at a distance without being so possessive that I was isolated. I saw other men regularly, and almost every night the Sergeant or my neighbors would come over to drink tea, chat, and listen to the radio. (The Sergeant listened to all the Arabic language programs broadcast by American, British, French, Russian, Libyan, Algerian, Moroccan, Chinese stations, switching the dial seriously from one to the next.) Things were going well. The complexities which revolved around establishing a fieldwork situation were now resolved. The anxiety-producing tensions of self-reflection temporarily eased as I involved myself in this external work.

After a month or so, there was a change in my relationship with the village. People seemed to accept me more as my initial strangeness was wearing off. This coincided with the first slackening of the inquiry process. We had completed our inventory of the ownership of fields and our initial sketch of the genealogies; much remained to be done, of course, but the outlines were there. The lists we had so diligently compiled were coming alive to me.

After the olive harvest—which absorbed everyone's energies for several weeks—was finished, the demands on me came pouring in again. Having fewer immediately obvious tasks to accomplish, and feeling the need for new villagers to work with, I acceded to more of these requests. This was a mistake; it reopened the floodgates of demand which I thought had been sealed. Now that we knew each other a little better, the limits were being tested again, in a more subtle manner, to see just how firm they really were.

Without my noticing it, Malik was becoming more nervous and irritable. It was clearer to him, I suppose, that since we had covered the initial ground, other more sensitive subjects could no longer be so easily avoided. He also felt that his grip on me was weakening. Although I was more than happy with him, I also insisted on working with other villagers.

I had been drawn into driving to Sefrou on two successive days by bogus if convincing requests. I was fed up with being used as a taxi driver and was feeling the need to get back to work. I was quite touchy and was beginning, for the first time since my arrival in the village, to feel frustrated again. I began to realize that this ease of interaction was too good to last. On the third day I intended to begin working on the saint's legend. Malik came in the mornings and was acting strangely diffident. Finally he announced, defiantly but defensively, that I had to drive him to the village of his wife's in-laws, some thirty kilometers away. He was having trouble with her (which he refused to talk about) and wanted to make a present to her relatives. He presented the matter as crucial, and there was no way to refuse him. He had planned this for several days, but observing my grouchiness about the taxi business he had hesitated to broach the subject.

Thinly masking my displeasure, I had some coffee with him and off we went. We drove to the village, paraded around a bit, had lunch, and started back. Fine, I said, back to work we go, no more rides. He agreed. When we pulled into the flat area in the center of the village there were two close cousins of his waiting for us. As I turned off the ignition they huddled with Malik. He turned to me as I was leaving the car and said that one of the wives was really sick and we had to take her to the doctor. I gave a sharp laugh and said, quite simply, No. "What would you have done before I was here? Whatever it was, do it now, because I am not going anywhere." There was embarrassment and consternation. The men from this sub-lineage had actually been restrained to the point of moderation in the requests they had made of me, and I knew that they were not likely to insist unnecessarily—which only increased my anger. But this time the emergency was real. So I agreed and everyone seemed relieved. They hurried off to assemble their womenfolk while Malik and I waited in the car. They brought out a young woman who was obviously dreadfully ill. I am not good with sick people, I was not sure of my driving, and I was thoroughly worn out. All the way to Sefrou she moaned for help; none was forthcoming. We dropped her off at a doctor who took one look at her and told us to take her to the hospital in Fez, another thirty kilometers away. Off we went, and after an hour of pulling strings at the hospital in Fez we managed to get her admitted. She died there a week later.

It was late in the afternoon when we got back in the car and started our trip back to Sidi Lahcen. I was silent and sullen. I was upset about the woman and exhausted and drained by the whole day. There was very little conversation. Finally we arrived in the village. I reassured an edgy Malik that everything was okay, not to worry, but I just wanted to be alone. I started to walk off in the direction of some outlying fields, and Malik followed. The Moroccans never really understood why anyone would want to take a walk by himself. I remembered my scene with Ali at the wedding; I had reached the limits of my endurance and could no longer maintain a good front. Malik persisted and persisted and so did I, until I finally turned to him and said slowly, firmly, and emphatically that I was not angry at him, that I was tired and wanted to be by myself. I would see him the following day. A look of dismay and hurt crossed his face. He said, *wash sekren?*—are you drunk?

I was stunned, speechless. We had been together every minute of the day since eight that morning. I knew that he meant something else and was himself deeply upset, but I was absolutely at the end of my emotional endurance. The infuriating irrationality of his comment threw me into a deeper depression, and made me wonder whether there had ever been any effective communication and understanding between us. I must have been deceiving myself; a vast gulf lay between us and could never be bridged. I felt on the edge of an abyss and had a rush of vertigo. Malik, in his own way, seemed also to have recognized a rupture. We followed the winding path back; he left me at my house with a gentle *lila sa'ida*, good evening.

After this incident, it was only with the greatest difficulty and pervasive emotional upset that I tried to determine whether the so-called emergencies were real. Whenever the Sergeant wanted to go to Sefrou I was happy to take him—both to repay him for his hospitality, and because practically no one was courageous enough to try to force his way into the car when he was present. He was not fond of Moroccans, as he would be glad to tell you or them.

It soon became apparent that unless something drastic were done about the car problem I would not do any fieldwork at all. The second week in the village I made four trips into Sefrou. After the fourth trip I seriously considered leaving the car in the city. I should have. When I returned to the village there was an old man waiting at the door of my one-room house. He said that his wife was very sick and had to get to the hospital. I said I was sorry, but I had just returned from Sefrou. He persisted, undaunted, in a tone of such distress and sincerity that I began to wonder if there wasn't a true emergency. I broke down and agreed. Off he went, returning with his old wife hobbling behind him. They thanked me profusely. We arrived in Sefrou and I stopped in front of the hospital. No, they said, a little higher up the street, the market. But didn't you say you were dying? Yes, she said, but I have some shopping to do.

I let them out and returned to the village knowing that that bridge had been crossed. I steadfastly refused after that incident. My anger was openly expressed on several occasions; persistent knockers at six in the morning were favorite targets. Force of character more than arguments carried the day, and the demands subsided. A few months later, after having a tune-up from a Moroccan *garagiste* friend, the car exploded.

I was finally rid of the wretched thing. The six-mile walk over rolling hills and across a shallow river to the nearest highway and gas station afforded me some of my most enjoyable and relaxing hours in

Morocco. The disappearance of the car also took a great deal of pressure off Malik, who it seems was approached by ten people for every intrepid villager who banged on my door. His life must have been hell.

*   *   *

This cathartic moment of realization was sobering for both of us, and led to a mutual stock-taking. Our work was slowing down and becoming less regular. This was highlighted during the next few weeks, when we began to do a series of household economies in depth. By now I had a fairly good abstract idea of the range of socio-economic variation in the village, and I wanted to find out what these differences in land holdings, income, and assets really meant in the daily life of the village families.

We worked first with the Sergeant, the richest man in the village, and found it surprisingly easy. He was proud of the holdings he had acquired, and candid about his future plans for expansion; this was the closest he came to being an informant. In working with other villagers, I soon found that even the poorest families were not reluctant to discuss and lament their economic situation. Poverty does not carry the stigma in Morocco which it does in America. It indicates only a lack of material goods at the present time, nothing more. Although regrettable, it does not reflect unfavorably on one's character. It simply means that Allah has not smiled on one, for reasons beyond normal understanding, but that things are bound to change soon.

Malik, neither rich nor poor, seemed to represent a "middle of the spectrum" position, and I proposed working on his holdings. He hesitated at first but then agreed. He had portrayed himself, to me and others, as a spiritual man of relative poverty. As we began to make a detailed list of his possessions, he became touchy and defensive. Listing all of his various small parcels of land, sheep, goats, and olive trees, it was clear that he was not nearly as impoverished as he had portrayed himself. By village standards, he was doing quite well.

This was confusing and troubling for him. He saw himself as having a difficult time in life. This was more than a ploy to coax money and sympathy from the anthropologist; it was truly an integral part of his identity. So, when he saw what was emerging on the paper in front of him, he was flustered. He had internalized a certain persona, and although in recent years his fortunes had improved—he had received his father's inheritance, and had two brothers working for him—his self-image had not changed.

The "facts" which were emerging did not correspond to his cultural categories. Moroccan villagers are not in the habit of totaling up their parcels of land, calculating their combined holdings, comparing them with the rising and falling prices of goods, and making systematic and quantitative comparisons with their neighbors. Nor do they understand their village conceptually in terms of socio-economic strata. There are, of course, societies (like our own) which do conceptualize social reality in such terms, but Morocco is not one of them. As he was objectifying his holdings for me, making them into a quantitative and external object which we could both examine, Malik began to see that there was a disparity between his self-image and my classification system. The emergence of this "hard" data before his eyes and through his own efforts was highly disconcerting for him.

Our objective social science, which treats facts as entities separable from a larger whole, is real enough for us (perhaps), but it was definitely foreign to Malik. He formed a more synthetic judgment of a man's situation, which turned on moral and social evaluations as much as on economic ones. The two poles of this conceptual scheme were those people for whom "things go well" (*nas la-bas 'ali-hom*) and "those for whom things are miserable" (*nas msakin*). These categories are total. For example, if a man has no sons, he is pitied (*meskine*), even if he is rich. A person's economic position was not ignored, it simply was not made the sole basis of the classification. Those who were "well-off" comprised perhaps one-quarter of the village in Malik's scheme. Those who were "poor, down trodden, to be pitied" comprised perhaps a third. As for the rest of the villagers, there was no special term to designate them, and this did not bother anyone. It was only under the prodding of the anthropologist that Malik tried to fit everyone into a particular stratum.

Malik was changing. He had to reformulate his own experiences in order to understand what I was driving at. Ordinarily he was quite adept at this, but when his own situation was the object, he faltered. After all, his new self-awareness stood in direct contradiction to his old self-image.

Whenever an anthropologist enters a culture, he trains people to objectify their life-world for him. Within all cultures, of course, there is already objectification and self-reflection. But this explicit self-conscious translation into an external medium is rare. The anthropologist creates a doubling of consciousness. Therefore, anthropological analysis must incorporate two facts: first, that we ourselves are historically situated through the questions we ask and the manner in which we seek to understand and experience the world; and second, that what we receive from our informants are interpretations, equally mediated by history and culture. Consequently, the data we collect is doubly mediated, first by our own presence and then by the second-order self-reflection we demand from our informants.

This by no means implies that cross-cultural understanding is impossible. So long as the different epistemological status of the data we receive is accounted for, it is not a block to understanding. Malik was not lying to me, nor was he simply being manipulative. He really did conceive of himself as *meskine*, not-well-off in a total sense. As we constructed an object together (a list of his holdings) he saw that he was relatively prosperous. He had to think carefully and deeply about this contradiction. His self-image was thrown into doubt. His naive consciousness was altered. He had never experienced himself as well-off. After reflecting on the matter for several days, he decided that his original judgment was correct. Yes, he had more land and sheep than most other villagers, but he had no father, his son was sickly, his mother needed support, his brothers were unmarried, and his uncle was out to steal his land. No, Monsieur Paul, things were tough. But a doubling of consciousness had occurred. Malik had been forced to look at his life in a new way. His world had new contours, even if his ultimate judgments about it were the same.

Much of the joking, bantering, and "sounding" which went on in the village was easy enough to handle. The one area where these demands and probes were not so easily brushed off, however, concerned jobs. Many of the men in their twenties and thirties had very little work to do. Under Islamic inheritance procedures, men do not inherit until the father dies, and in this village there was not that much to inherit in most cases anyway. Holdings were small and there was plenty of dead time between farm tasks. The men joked and complained about their situation frequently. In my presence, these laments often turned into requests for my help in finding them jobs in France. Three villagers had in fact found work as agricultural laborers in France. They regularly sent money home, which enabled them to acquire land, improve their houses, marry off their sons, and strut around in sunglasses and suits when they visited. They aroused pervasive envy, but the onlookers had little to do but grumble.

I knew by now that the possibilities of further agricultural expansion in this region had been reached. These men's perceptions were accurate; their future was not bright. There was no industry in Sefrou, and the only real path of mobility out of the village was the educational system—and even the opportunities for taking that route were rapidly disappearing as the flood of job openings in the state bureaucracy after independence were now largely filled.

Each request from the men gathered in front of one of the ramshackle stores, sitting in the dirt, full of energy but with no outlet except fighting and squabbling, persuasively communicated their anxiety. The plight of these men was real enough.

In the early stages of fieldwork, the anthropologist operates with his own version of "naive consciousness." The reality "out there" seems so concrete, so easy to gather in. My exhilaration during the initial months in the village was tied to this sureness. There was not much to interpret; the facts seemed to speak for themselves once they were collected. Taking the external world as it appears is an essential first step; it is gratifying, easy to hold onto but inadequate.

Actually, what the "facts" demonstrated was far from obvious. If all they showed was that Morocco was a Third World country with underemployment and a rather unpromising economic future, then there was no need to have journeyed there in the first place. I had known that much in Chicago. This does not mean that generalizations at this level are either wrong or unnecessary. French colonialism and neo-colonialism are deeply connected to Morocco's current problems. But at this level of generality, these guiding ideas are almost empty.

What at first seem to be the broadest and richest concepts, capable of organizing and clarifying the most material turn out to be the most impoverished. The passage from broad assertions—that neo-colonialism is the cause of rural poverty in Morocco, for example—to individual cases must be mediated by particular determinations, because otherwise there is no way to differentiate one village from the next, one country from another. I began to realize this as the outlines of village history became clearer. Yes, the poverty in Sidi Lahcen was largely the result of the French Protectorate. Yet a neighboring village, similarly impoverished today, had actually prospered under French rule. The impact of the French Protectorate was undeniable, yet it varied greatly even within this one region.

At the turn of the century, Sidi Lahcen Lyussi had been a prosperous village. It had bountiful water and an irrigation system which was more than adequate for its needs. The village was a religious center for the tribes. Leaders of the saintly lineages played an active role in mediating tribal disputes. This increased both the prestige and the wealth of the village as a whole. Even when the French moved in to establish military control in the countryside (before the First World War), the chief mediator in the village was prevailed upon to serve as a go-between with the tribes.

The French acknowledge the predominant role of Sidi Lahcen. In fact, shortly after the First World War they offered to build a military academy, market, and school complex adjacent to the village. The village elders, fearing that this would undermine the religious education of their children, refused the offer. The French, in accord with their policy of trying to avoid obviously coercive measures, accepted the refusal and built the complex in another village some miles away. That village is today quite prosperous.

This was really the beginning of a basic and overall decline for the inhabitants of Sidi Lahcen. Their religious authority was undercut by the emergence of the French courts, which, having less legitimacy, were easier for the Berbers to manipulate. As their mediating role declined, their spiritual reputation sank.

By turning inward, they also gradually closed off the possibility of economic growth. At the time of the First World War, there was more than enough land for the population; in fact, a great deal of acreage was not under cultivation at all. Gradually, over the next fifty years, this good fortune changed. Population grew rapidly. The government reclaimed a certain amount of land for reforestation programs. Land which had been used as communal grazing land was parcelled out. Alternatives grew scarce. The impact of these long-term changes, however, did not make itself felt in an immediate and drastic fashion.

Not until the 1960s was the situation clear enough for everyone to see. The village made an attempt to capture the new Rural Commune Council headquarters for itself. It would have brought with it a market, paved road, electricity, some graft, and a reinvigoration of village life—all things which the majority of the villagers now sought. They lost out on their bid, however; internal squabbling rendered them indecisive at a key meeting, and another village was chosen. That village, not very far from Sidi Lahcen, is today doing quite well for itself. The villagers see this and are bitter. They now realize that the future possibilities of expansion for them are almost nil. Their lucidity about their condition serves only to aggravate their lives. They have little to do but sit and grumble. As one man called out to me, "We'll all have to go to Paris—right, Monsieur Paul?"

What seemed, to my own naive consciousness, to "speak for itself" proved to be the most in need of interpretation. In this instance, the economic conditions could only be understood when the history of the religious, social, ecological, political, and psychodynamic determinations were brought into play. The problem was to connect my abstract concepts with the immediately perceived realities of everyday village life. This could only be done by tracing particular mediations, which otherwise would remain sterile truisms. The rest of my fieldwork was devoted to that task.

6. Transgression

After the first several months, my work in Sidi Lahcen was more painstakingly fragmentary and less immediately gratifying. During long, uneventful stretches I struggled with the increasingly imperative need to begin synthesizing my material, formulating specific questions, and searching for ways to answer them. Lévi-Strauss has said that if anthropology was adventure, then he was adventure's bureaucrat. I began to understand what he meant.

In the months which followed, I spent a great many hours merely wandering around the village and its fields, engaging in casual talk while sitting around the stores, setting up interviews, waiting for informants, and just being bored. My Arabic was considerably better by this time. I tried to maintain a regular work schedule with Malik and several other villagers, but this proved difficult. One particularly trying afternoon when I was cajoling Malik into discussing the local political activity against the French, he became exasperated with my persistent questions and said I was squeezing him like an olive press: if you squeeze too hard, you get the pulp but not the best oil.

After the months of consistently self-absorbing

activity, I knew I had passed a threshold of acceptance. Slowly and sporadically, I was moving toward the kind of understanding I was seeking. Unlike library research, field data was fixed once one
had left. Thus the further along I was, the more I
questioned myself as to the state of the data. Particularly toward the end of the stay, I might have to
search for weeks for someone who had the knowledge of a specific subject and the willingness to discuss it with me. If I failed to find such a person and
convince him to work with me, I was out of luck.
There would be a gap and there was no way to fill it
back in Chicago. I awoke each morning with the
sense that the material was there if only I could
figure out a way to get at it. But as Malik put it, there
was only one door open to me—patience, only patience.

An inverse ratio began to develop between time
invested in specific questions and the accessibility of
a response. New informants (whom one often had
to cajole into just coming to talk) would be unfamil-
iar with my methods of work and modes of questioning. There was no possibility of investing the
time necessary to cultivate and train a major informant for each point of information. But this in no
way changed the fact that delicacy and ritualized
politesse were demanded by the situation.

A wider net had to be cast. It met resistance
from Malik and others, for political, economic, and
merely habitual reasons. I was helped to make another forward movement by two incidents (partly
accidental, partly of my own engineering) which
helped me over some important hurdles and shored

up my confidence in pursuing the inquiry more vigorously.

During this period, Ali came out to the village for a rest cure. He had a bad case of scabies, which is quite common in this part of Morocco. Many of the school children are afflicted with it, losing their hair and being covered with sores. It is ugly, uncomfortable, and annoying, but otherwise not serious. Although it is easily cured, I was told by the local French doctor that the Moroccan government had refused to issue sufficient import licenses for medication.

I confided to Ali one night that I was having difficulty getting people to talk about political events during the exile of the sultan some fifteen years earlier. I was sure that the consequences of this extremely divisive period must still play a role in current village politics. Ali concurred. He agreed to break the conspiracy of silence if I would drive him into Sefrou to see his mistress. I readily consented.

The event which triggered and then catalyzed resistance to the French Protectorate, and which culminated in independence for Morocco, was the forced exile of the sultan. Mohammed V had been originally chosen by the French because they thought he would be docile. But over the years, he gradually became converted to the nationalist cause. In the early nineteen fifties he made several speeches and statements which the French used as an excuse to oust him. With the aid of several famous Berber *qaids* in the south, the French started a predominantly rural-based movement which culminated in his exile and replacement by a puppet sultan.

In Sidi Lahcen, the villagers (particularly the saint's descendants) were caught in an acutely uncomfortable bind. They had been closely allied with a powerful *qaid* in the region who was a supporter of the French. During the exile they were pressured to support this *qaid* and the French by pronouncing the weekly prayers in the name of the new sultan, which amounted to legitimating the French action. At the same time, there were also anti-French groups and a guerrilla army in the region who made demands for supplies and security. A few villagers joined these groups, while a few openly backed the exile. Most of the rest were caught in between. All in all, it was a period of tremendous tension which many of the villagers would rather forget. It had particularly important consequences, however, since the political alignments during the exile period played a key role in the regional power struggles which followed independence. The role of groups, individuals, and factions in these events could only be properly understood against the background of the exile period. And I had to understand more about this period if I were to make sense of more recent developments. But everyone seemed extremely reluctant to talk in specifics; even those who were on the winning side were hesitant to reopen this Pandora's box of strife and bitterness.

Ali told me his version of the events in great detail and with great relish. The fights, betrayals, fears, and reprisals which marked the period were listed and embellished in his own inimitable style. Although many of the points had to be reevaluated later, Ali's story did provide me with the essential outlines of what had happened and who was on what side. Once Malik and others found out that Ali had told me his version of the events, their historical amnesia was quickly overcome; they were appalled, knowing full well what tales Ali was capable of inventing. Suddenly I found cooperation on these matters strikingly easy to achieve; their own counter-versions were presented almost matter-of-factly. Feigning indifference, people provided details as if this were a trivial subject.

Once the silence was broken, once a partisan account was given, other individuals and factions felt it incumbant upon themselves to protect their own interests by telling their version. There followed, over the next months, a series of interviews, some open, other stealthily held at night—ample proof that the wounds were still tender and fear of the government still alive.

Similar incidents occurred at other times during the fieldwork. Respecting their resistance would have constituted a major stumbling block. Recasting my work, however, would have provided me with no assurance of avoiding future dead ends. In fact such compliance on my part might have encouraged them to construct new obstacles. My response was essentially an act of violence; it was carried out on a symbolic level, but it was violence nonetheless. I was transgressing the integrity of my informants by obtaining information from Ali (who was certainly using it against them). I knew this would coerce, almost blackmail, the others into exposing aspects of their lives which they had thus far passionately shielded from me. I was intruding beyond the boundaries which were acceptable and comfortable. For Ali to do this, of course, was one thing. He consciously and explicitly sought to make the villagers squirm, relishing the prospect. But he was himself open to attack on this issue, and it goes without saying that attacks were forthcoming. The stakes for me were in no way comparable, and the villagers could not retaliate except through various forms of passive resistance.

Malik had been presenting me with a sort of official discourse. Once Ali violated the text, the very story of discord and strife which the villagers had been suppressing was re-enacted in a minor key. Without Ali or the equivalent—someone close enough to the group to know its intimate antagonisms but also independent enough not to care much about protecting the sensibilities of the community and far enough removed not to fear reprisals—the anthropologist would have been successfully blocked. Ali's actions allowed me to continue my research in the way I wanted to pursue it.

To those who claim that some form of this symbolic violence was not part of their own field experience, I reply simply that I do not believe them. It is inherent in the structure of the situation. This is not to say that every anthropologist is aware of it, for sensibilities differ. The form and intensity no doubt vary greatly, but they are all variations on a common theme.

7. Self-Consciousness

As the months rolled by, so did the major celebrations of the Islamic year. During Ramadan, the lunar month of fasting, I had many discussions with different people about its meaning—how they felt about it personally, changes in it from earlier periods, and so on. Villagers were relatively open about what one could call standard Islam. The same held true for the Koran itself. Although Malik and others in the village actually understand very little about the complexities of the text, there was no hesitation about discussing it with me. On school vacations, for example, when my neighbor's son or other young men attending the Karawiyin University in Fez returned to Sidi Lahcen, Malik and I and others would gather and listen to their explanations of the Koran proper, of the *hadith* or traditional commentaries, and of some of the current dilemmas facing the Islamic world.

We even discussed Ali and the Aissawa. This was touchier because of the bad blood between Ali and so many of the other villagers. Nonetheless, I had little trouble broaching the subject, at least in general terms, of the various brotherhoods in Sefrou, their relative merits and the local stereotyping of their members.

Strangely enough, the one area of religion about

131

which the villagers proved to be extremely reluctant
to talk concerned their own saint, Sidi Lahcen
Lyussi. I knew that a legend had grown up about
him, and nothing seemed safer than to ask his descendants about his exploits and *baraka*. In fact, I
largely viewed our discussions of standard Islam as a
prelude to delving into the particular form Islam took
in this rural village. My inquiries over the months
were met with feet shuffling, short replies, and a
general sense that this was not something that
people were eager to talk about. I rarely pursued the
subject after the second or third rebuff, but I began to
be intrigued by their reticence. Finally, after a relatively long period in the village, it became clear that
one of the chief reasons for their embarrassment was
that even the saint's descendants themselves did not
know very much about their progenitor. Malik, for
example, although he had been a *fqi,* read classical
Arabic only with the greatest difficulty. Sidi Lariou-
sahcen's more technical treatises on poetry, logic,
and metaphysics were unquestionably beyond his
ken. Actually it had never really occurred to Malik to
try to read them.

I was not surprised that little was known about
the historical person, but there was also a general
ignorance of his legend. Bits and scraps of it were
commonly known, one or two incidents, but there
were no occasions when the legend was recited as a
whole. Nor were there any specialists who were
charged with remembering it. During the fieldwork
villagers became acutely aware that they did not
know their saint's legend and they now felt that

they should. Men from the saintly lineages apparently collected and pieced together various tales which people knew about. Gradually Malik assembled these and we eventually had something resembling a legend, much to the gratification of the anthropologist, who also felt a strong need to have one.

Our prodding apparently stimulated some interest in the historical saint himself. Some of the students in Fez started to ask around in the bookstores there for his works, several of which were still extant. I bought two myself, but one in the village could quite read them. There was an almost total ignorance about the children of Sidi Lahcen or the history of the descendants until the turn of the current century.

This process of rediscovery of the villagers' heritage was an interesting one to watch, once I realized what was going on. Here, it was not that people were resisting or hiding something from me, but that they were embarrassed by their own ignorance; also, my questions were not considered bizarre. The bitter irony of this heathen foreigner stimulating them to ask questions about their own spiritual heritage was not lost on them.

During the course of the year there were several occasions on which groups would come to the village to visit the saint's tomb. Anyone was free to come to the saint and ask favors of him at any time. In return, they would usually bring an offering ranging from a candle to a sheep. Whatever alms were collected were divided equally among the

Sidi Lahcen Lyussi: Berber horsemen come to honor the saint.

members of the saintly lineages (an insignificant amount economically). Group visits to the saint were more highly organized, and I fully expected that at least here I would be able to see local Islam in action, with or without explanations. The two major events of the year are the *musem*-s, or celebrations in honor of the saint. The smaller *musem* is held in the spring before the harvest. The major one takes place in the fall after the harvest, when tribal groups from the entire region come to Sadi Lahcen for three full days of singing, feasting, and visiting friends. The famous Berber fantasia in which teams of resplendent horsemen vie with each other in displays of Berber poetry and horseback riding climaxes the festival.

In addition to these two celebrations, there are several special tribal groups who come each year to pay their respects to the saint. One of these groups is from the neighboring tribe of the Beni Yarghra. This is an Arabic-speaking tribe whose territory is immediately adjacent to the Berber-speaking groups of Ait Youssi and Ait Helli which surround the village. I was able to learn little about the historical development of this relationship, or even about the legendary accounts of how it formed. Apparently there was a chapter of a small brotherhood which owed allegiance to Sidi Lahcen. In typical Moroccan fashion it was an isolated unit, locally based, displaying little interest in the activities of other groups.

The visit of this tribal group to Sidi Lahcen, only a few weeks after the smaller *musem*, was my first opportunity to observe a major interaction of the

tribal groups and the saintly lineages. I eagerly
awaited their arrival. But the saint's descendants
were less than ebullient about the forthcoming visit.
The same reserve and studied disinterest applied to
all of the other events, including the two *musem*-s.
This intrigued me. In a small mountain village, with
great underemployment and an abundance of spare
time, I would have thought that any diversion
would have been anticipated with some pleasure.
The anthropologist certainly welcomed a change in
the daily routine. But such was not the case for the
villagers.

The Beni Yarghra, the neighboring tribal group,
could be seen from quite a distance as they approached Sidi Lahcen. The central area of the village
overlooks the valley below it and the ridges and
valleys beyond that. One could see the group of
some seventy or eighty people several kilometers
away. They were led by an old man who carried a
banner of tattered green cloth. He was the head of
the lodge and was more than willing to talk later,
though he had little detail to fill in. Following him
were men, women, and children, some riding on
donkeys and mules, some just striding along as the
procession made its way up the valley through the
olive trees. As they drew closer one could hear their
chanting. The *dikr*, or litany, of the brotherhood was
a set of simple phrases asking Sidi Lahcen for his
blessing. It was repeated time and time again, an
end in itself. Just behind the man carrying the banner was another who was leading a cow which
would be a ritual offering to the saint. As the group
reached the beaten earth of the *musem* area in front

of the mosque and tomb, the chanting increased in volume and perhaps twenty or thirty of the men from the saintly lineages assembled to meet the visitors. People shook hands, embraced, and then both groups joined in a forceful set of litanies and proceeded to the interior of the tomb. Here they would receive tea and some food. This is a reversal of the *musem* pattern in which the visitors bring food to feed the saint's descendants. A fight had been simmering for the last few years as to which sub-lineage ought to provide the tea, which the stews, and which the bread. One year, apparently, a fight had broken out and no one had prepared any food. This was considered shocking and a cause of displeasure for the saint. This year, group solidarity was hardly at a peak, but relationships had been patched up enough so that at least tea and food could be presented to the visitors.

After a period of relaxation and casual talk, it was time to slaughter the cow. The spokesman for the Beni Yarghra apologized for the size of the animal (which was rather small), saying it was not like the old days when everyone contributed. The cow was untied and led around to the back of the mosque, next to a large cement basin, built by the government, at the point where the mountain springs emerge. A few verses of the Koran were recited in preparation for the sacrifice of the cow. The man from Sidi Lahcen in charge, however, bungled the job: he did not manage to cut deeply enough to kill the cow. The cow bellowed in pain and rage. Kicking furiously and gushing blood from its half-severed neck, it broke away from the man who was

The botching of a ritual offering caused much anxiety.

holding it and rushed headlong down the path in front of it. A mad scramble followed as twenty or thirty men and what seemed like a hundred *drari* chased after it screaming, yelling, and brandishing knives. Finally, after what felt like a very long time indeed, they caught the cow and succeeded in hacking its head off. Blood was everywhere, for the cow had run in crazed circles. It was dragged back to the basin, where everyone tried to regain their composure, without much success. The parcelling out of the meat to the appropriate sub-lineages was carried out in relative silence during the rest of the afternoon. Meat, and particularly beef, is a rarity for these villagers. Most villagers will not eat meat more than once a week and many only once a month. When a cow is being slaughtered in the village, men from the surrounding countryside will drift in and watch the parcelling and auctioning process, which can take an entire afternoon to accomplish. No one misses it. There is always a highly animated discussion, and the piles of red meat and guts in the center of the *musem* area have an almost aphrodisical effect. The near silence on this particular afternoon was a startling contrast.

That night, Malik corralled the leader of the brotherhood and several other visitors and we had them over for dinner. They were surprisingly open and voluble with me but had little concrete "ethnographic" detail to offer. They were repeatedly apologetic to Malik about the paucity of the offerings they were bringing; Malik was suitably haughty.

They left the next day. The delegation assembled in front of the mosque and did some chanting with the assembled villagers, minus the cow. They then proceeded to walk slowly away from the tomb out of the village. They walked backwards so as to avoid turning their backs on the saint, chanting all the while. It was only several hundred yards down the valley that they turned around and continued on their way.

The next night I was invited to have dinner at Malik's house. This happened only rarely during my stay, and so I knew that this was a special occasion. When I arrived at his simple dwelling, assembled in the one room were also several of the more successful and powerful men from Malik's sublineage. These men were not the village elders. In fact, they were in their forties and fifties. However, they were all teachers of Arabic and one was even the school superintendent for the region. They had always been cordial and cooperative with me, if distant. Clearly they were the power group who had finally given the green light for my entry, and clearly they had at least approved of Malik's working with me. He had great respect for them and treated them deferentially.

During the dinner we chatted about this and that—about my stay, about how I found the food, the weather, and the olive harvest. Malik said almost nothing, which was unusual for him. Finally, after dinner and while we were drinking several obligatory cups of mint tea, they began mentioning Sidi Lahcen, in a roundabout way. These men could all read classical Arabic with some facility. They had, of course, been informed of the questions I had been asking over the previous months, and it had set them to thinking. They explained this all to me in serious and surprisingly non-defensive tones. They said that they knew very little about their saint, except that his *baraka* (divine power) and learning made even the greatest of Sultans tremble. But that *baraka* had been lost over the years. Monsieur Paul, the superintendent said, we are nothing but withered grapes on the great vine of Sidi Lahcen.

Their acute self-consciousness and unflinching judgment of their spiritual condition was presented in a quiet, almost weary tone. Their discomfort at the sight of the cow running through the village with its head half-off had shamed them deeply. Their divine grace was gone, and there was nothing they could do about it. Materially these men were doing well, they were prosperous. But the very deepest core of their identity, the symbol on which their sense of worth turned, was their position as descendants of Sidi Lahcen. It was clear for all to see that the erosion of that identity was severe.

8. Friendship

Driss ben Mohammed, a jovial, portly, and even-tempered young man, had consistently refused to work as an informant. Over the course of my stay we had come to know each other casually, as time permitted, almost accidentally. Gradually, a certain trust had flowered between us. At its root, I think, was an awareness of our differences and a mutual respect.

Ben Mohammed was not afraid of me (as many other villagers were), nor did he have hesitations about associating with Europeans (although he had had almost no personal contact with them), nor did he seek to profit from my presence (he refused most gifts). Simply, he was my host and treated me with the respect which is supposed to be reserved for a guest, even one who stayed as long as I did.

To be friends, according to Aristotle, two people "must be mutually recognized as bearing goodwill and wishing well to each other . . . either because of utility, pleasure, or good. . . . That type of friendship stemming from the good is best because . . . that which is good without qualification is also pleasant, but such friendships require time and familiarity . . . a wish for friendship may arise quickly but friendship does not."*

*Nicomachean Ethics, Book VIII, Chapter 2, p. 1060 in The Basic Works of Aristotle, edited by Richard McKeon (Random House, New York, 1941).

As time wore on and my friendship with ben Mohammed deepened, I was learning more and more from him. During the last months of fieldwork, when he was home from school and we could spend many of the hot hours together, the field experience, now nearing its completion, reached a new emotional and intellectual depth. Casually, without plan or schedule, just walking around the fields, ripe with grain or muddy from the irrigation water in the truck gardens, we had a meandering series of conversations. Ben Mohammed's initial refusal of informant status set up the possibility of another type of communication. But clearly our communication would not have been possible without those more regularized and disciplined relationships I had had with others. Partly in reaction to the professional situation, we had slipped into a more unguarded and relaxed course over the months.

Although we talked of many things, perhaps the most significant set of discussions turned on our relations to our separate traditions. It would have been almost impossible to have had such conversations with either Ali or Malik, emmeshed as they were in the web of their own local world. Nor, for that matter, would it have been possible with many of the Frenchified Moroccan intellectuals; half torn out of their own ill-understood traditions, and afflicted with a heightened and unhappy self-consciousness, they would be unable to bridge the gap either way. Ben Mohammed, in his own modest way, was also an intellectual, but he was one of those who still looked to Fez rather than Paris for his inspiration. This provided a crucial space between us.

The fundamental tenet of Islam, for ben Mohammed, was that all believers are equal before Allah, even though pride, egoism, and ignorance obscure this fact. Very, very, few people, in his view, actually believe in Islam. Most take only a "narrow" view: they think that if they merely follow the basic pre- scriptions then they are Muslims. Ben Mohammed emphatically disagreed. If belief in the equality among believers and in submission to Allah is not in your heart, and does not inform your actions, then prayer or even the pilgrimage to Mecca counts for nothing. *Niya*, or intention, is the key. You might be able to fool your neighbors by shallow adherence to externals, but you would not fool Allah. Today, for ben Mohammed, the true Muslim is mistrusted in the Islamic world. People interpret generosity and submission as weakness or foolishness. Boasting, hypocrisy, quarreling, and fighting prevail because people do not truly understand and accept the wis- dom of Islam.

He brought up the example of Sidi Lahcen. Most of the saint's descendants knew little if anything about his teachings or his "path." They are ignorant. Yet they feel superior to other Muslims because they are descended from a famous saint and can lay claim to his *baraka*, to his holiness. But if they would read the books which their patron saint wrote, they would see that Sidi Lahcen himself fought against such vanity. He had preached submission to Allah alone. The only true nobles in Islam were those who lived exemplary lives and followed Allah. Sidi Lahcen's descendants, however, by relying on his spiritual strength, had lost their own. They think that their genealogical connections alone should command re- spect; Sidi Lahcen would have disagreed.

Ben Mohammed was striving, he said, to follow the path of Sidi Lahcen. But it posed specific prob-lems for him. His father, whom he respected, ve-hemently opposed his "reformist" interpretations. This would not change ben Mohammed's personal beliefs, but it was his duty to respect those of his father. Ben Mohammed knew that his father, an old man set in his ways, was not about to alter his views. Actually, Sidi Lahcen himself had taken a parallel stance in his own age: popular religion was to be combatted in its excesses but tolerated for its piety.

For ben Mohammed the tensions of his world view turned on these two Moroccan alternatives. Moroc-co's future was far from bright. He would have great difficulty in finding the kind of work and life he de-sired. His expectations were geared to those of his country. But he also knew that the symbols and guides for the future would have to be drawn from Morocco's tradition. Moroccans could not ignore the West. This attitude required borrowing, integrating, and eliminating certain archaic and oppressive prac-tices, but it did not mean merely imitating the West; and most important of all, it did not require the abandonment of Islam.

With most informants, I would have stopped at this point of generality. But with ben Mohammed I felt I could proceed further. Throughout my stay in Morocco I had noticed that black was negatively val-ued in a variety of ways. In the broadest terms, white was generally equated with good and black with evil. Malik in particular seemed consistently concerned about color distinctions and their symbolism. Black was bad, according to his view, a color worthy of a dog. The lighter you are the better you are, the more you shone in the eyes of Allah. Malik was joking one day about a very poor villager. He said the man was so poor he would have to marry a black. Malik's new-born daughter, he pointed out innumerable times, was very white. When I showed him pictures of America he always made a point of saying that he could not tell if the blacks were men or women. He had been very upset when he found out that one of his favorite songs on the radio was by a black group. After that, he was careful to find out the color of a singer before offering any opinions on the music. Malik was not at all timid about discussing this symbolism. He was quite sure of himself; his source of ultimate authority was the Koran.

Throughout my stay I had been the dutiful anthropologist and noted down his comments, refraining from publicly reacting. But toward the end I let myself be affected by them more, and they really began to rankle. I am light in complexion with blue eyes and light brown hair. I was tempted many times to ask Malik, who has a dark skin tone, kinky hair, and large lips, if he thought this made me superior to him, but I never did. There was no point in confronting him.

Ben Mohammed was a different story. When I finally approached him about my feelings on the matter, he was quite lucid. We were sitting on a hillside, under some fig trees, overlooking the Breughalesque field below, amiably passing a hot, cloudless summer afternoon. I cautiously began to unburden myself about Malik. Again ben Mohammed straddled the cultural divide rather artfully. He fully agreed that the downgrading of blacks was a bad thing. It was incumbent on Muslims to fight racism in all its forms. There was no ambiguity on that point. But, such symbolism was indeed in the Koran. Most people rely on custom and not on their own intelligence. Malik was a peasant and could not be expected to know any better. He had been raised with these aphorisms, and lived with them, and he was not going to easily rid himself of such a bias.

He cautioned me, however, not to confuse Malik's views with the kind of racism he knew existed in America or Europe. Although Malik expressed anti-black sentiments, no Moroccan would ever keep someone out of a hotel or a job because of his skin color. Cultures were different, ben Mohammed was saying. Even when they say the same thing, an expression can mean something entirely different when it is played out in society. Be careful about your judgments. I agreed.

Yet, there was one further question to ask: Are we all equal, ben Mohammed? Or are Muslims superior? He became flustered. Here there was no possibility of reformist interpretation or compromise. The answer was no, we are not equal. All Muslims, even the most unworthy and reprehensible, and we named a few we both knew, are superior to all non-Muslims. That was Allah's will. The division of the world into Muslim and non-Muslim was *the* fundamental cultural distinction, the Archimedean point from which all else turned. This was ultimately what separated us. But, as Aristotle points out, "in a friendship based on virtue, complaints do not arise, but the purpose of the doer is a sort of measure; for in purpose lies the essential element of virtue and character . . . friend-

ship asks a man to do what he can, not what is pro-
portional to the merits of the case, since that can not
always be done. . . ."*

The lessons of tolerance and self-acceptance which
ben Mohammed had been teaching me during the
past months held sway. I had a strong sense of being
American. I knew it was time to leave Morocco.

*   *   *

The "revolution" had occurred during my absence
(1968-1969). My friends from Chicago, many of them
now living in New York, were fervently and un-
abashedly "political" when I returned. New York,
where I had grown up, looked the same as when I
had left it. But the city and my friends were now
more impenetrable to me than ben Mohammed. The
whole revery of future *communitas* which had sustained me through months of loneliness refused to
actualize itself upon my return. I adopted a stance of
passivity waiting for it to appear. Perhaps the most
bizarre dimension of my return was the fact that my
friends were now seemingly preoccupied with the
Third World; at least the phrase had an obligatory
place in their discourse. I had just been in the Third
World with a vengeance. Yet this Third World which
they so avidly portrayed bore no obvious relation to
my experiences. Initially when I pointed this out, I
was politely ignored. When I persisted it was
suggested that I was perhaps a bit reactionary. The
maze of slightly blurred nuance, that feeling of barely
grasped meanings which had been my constant
companion in Morocco overtook me once again. But
now I was home.

Nicomachean Ethics, Book VIII, Chapter 13, p. 1075 in McKeon.

Over the next several years other activities absorbed me, writing and teaching among them. Writing this book seems to have enabled me to go on to another type of fieldwork, to begin again on a different terrain.

Trinh Van Du entered the room carrying a dozen roses for our hostess. He was perhaps five feet tall and drew attention to this immediately by announcing that although he was thirty-three, Americans often mistook him for fifteen. The first hour or so of introductory chat was a bit stilted, but Du managed to include six or seven references to Ho Chi Minh along with the fact that he had been in the United States almost twelve years, doing odd jobs and teaching, for a time, at the Monterey Army language school. Things warmed up enormously when we switched from politics and credentials to language and culture. Yes, he would love to teach us Vietnamese and introduce us to Vietnamese literature, particularly poetry. The Hue dialect, his own, is the most poetic (as are its women), the Saigon dialect the most sing-song like Chinese, and the Hanoi the most precise and clear. But all Vietnamese read the same language and all love the *Tale of Kieu*. He would recite it for us in all three dialects and we would choose the one we liked best. Leaping up, filled with sparkle, yet almost solemn, he recited the first verses of the famous nineteenth-century poem, three times.

Conclusion

Culture is interpretation. The 'facts' of anthropology, the material which the anthropologist has gone to the field to find, are already themselves interpretations. The baseline data is already culturally mediated by the people whose culture we, as anthropologists, have come to explore. Facts are made—the word comes from the Latin *factum*, "made"—and the facts we interpret are made and remade. Therefore they cannot be collected as if they were rocks, picked up and put into cartons and shipped home to be analyzed in the laboratory.

Culture in all of its manifestations is overdetermined. It does not present itself neutrally or with one voice. Every cultural fact can be interpreted in many ways, both by the anthropologist and by his subjects. The scientific revolutions which established these parameters at the turn of the current century have been largely ignored in anthropology. Frederic Jameson's reference to the paradigm shift in linguistics applies to anthropology as well. He notes "a movement from a substantive way of thinking to a relational one. . . . Difficulties arose from terms which tried to name substances or objects . . . while linguistics was a science characterized by the absence of such substances. . . . There are first of all

points of view . . . with whose help you then sub-
sequently create your objects."*

The fact that all cultural facts are interpretations,
and multivocal ones at that, is true both for the anthropologist and for his informant, the Other with
whom he works. His informant—and the word is
accurate—must interpret his own culture and that of
the anthropologist. The same holds for the anthropologist. Both live in rich, partially integrated, on-
going life worlds. They are, however, not the same.
Nor is there any mechanical and easy means of translation from one set of experiences to the other. That
problem and the process of translation, therefore,
become one of the central arts and crucial tasks of
fieldwork. It should be clear that the view of the
"primitive" as a creature living by rigid rules, in total
harmony with his environment, and essentially not
cursed with a glimmer of self-consciousness, is a set
of complex cultural projections. There is no "primitive." There are other men, living other lives.

Anthropology is an interpretive science. Its object
of study, humanity encountered as Other, is on the
same epistemological level as it is. Both the anthropologist and his informants live in a culturally
mediated world, caught up in "webs of signification" they themselves have spun. This is the ground
of anthropology; there is no privileged position, no
absolute perspective, and no valid way to eliminate
consciousness from our activities or those of others.

*Frederic Jameson, *The Prison House of Language* (Princeton University Press, Princeton, 1972), p. 13.

This central fact can be avoided by pretending it does not exist. Both sides can be frozen. We can pretend that we are neutral scientists collecting unambiguous data and that the people we are studying are living amid various unconscious systems of determining forces of which they have no clue and to which only we have the key. But it is only pretense.

Anthropological facts are cross-cultural, because they are made across cultural boundaries. They exist as lived experience, but they are made into facts during the process of questioning, observing, and experiencing—which both the anthropologist and the people with whom he lives engage in. This means that the informant must first learn to explicate his own culture, to become self-conscious about it and begin to objectify his own life-world. He must then learn to "present" it to the anthropologist, to an outsider who by definition does not understand even the most obvious things. This presentation by the informant is defined, therefore, by being in a mode of externality. The informant is asked in innumerable ways to think about particular aspects of his own world, and he must then learn to construct ways to present this newly focused-on object to someone who is outside his culture, who shares few of his assumptions, and whose purpose and procedures are opaque. Thus when a Moroccan describes his lineage structure to an anthropologist, he must do several things. He must first become self-reflective and self-conscious about certain aspects of his life which he had previously taken largely for granted. Once he arrives at some understanding of what the anthropologist is driving at, thinks about that subject matter, and comes to a conclusion (all of which can occur in a matter of seconds, of course, and is not in itself a theoretical process), the informant must then figure out how to present this information to the anthropologist, an outsider who is by definition external to his usual life-world.

This creates the beginnings of a hybrid, cross-cultural object or product. During the period of fieldwork a system of shared symbols must be developed if this process of object formation—through self-reflection, self-objectification, presentation, and further explication—is to continue. Particularly in its early stages when there is little common experience, understanding, or language to fall back on, this is a very difficult and trying process; the ground is just not there. Things become more secure as this liminal world is mutually constructed but, by definition, it never really loses its quality of externality. This externality, however, is a moving ratio. It is external both for the anthropologist (it is not his own life-world) and for the informants, who gradually learn to inform. The present somewhat nasty connotations of the word do apply at times, but so does its older root sense "to give form to, to be the formative principle of, to animate." What is given form is this communication. The informant gives external form to his own experiences, by presenting them to meet the anthropologist's questions, to the extent that he can interpret them.

This informing, however, goes on not in a laboratory but in interpersonal interaction. It is intersubjective, between subjects. At best, it is partial and thin. The depth and scope of the culture that has been constructed is often woefully inadequate when measured against people interacting and carrying on their daily rounds in the everyday world. Anthropology is not a set of questionnaires which are handed over, filled out, and handed back. Most of the anthropologist's time is spent sitting around waiting for informants, doing errands, drinking tea, taking genealogies, mediating fights, being pestered for rides, and vainly attempting small talk—all in someone else's culture. The inadequacy of one's comprehension is incessantly brought to the surface and publicly displayed.

Interruptions and eruptions mock the fieldworker and his inquiry; more accurately, they may be said to inform his inquiry, to be an essential part of it. The constant breakdown, it seems to me, is not just an annoying accident but a core aspect of this type of inquiry. Later I became increasingly aware that these ruptures of communication were highly revealing, and often proved to be turning points. At the time, however, they seemed only to represent our frustration. Etymology comes to the rescue again: *e-ruption*, a breaking out, and *inter-ruption*, a breaking in, of this liminal culture through which we were trying to communicate.

Whenever these breaks occurred—and I have described several of the most important ones earlier—the cycle began again. This cross-cultural communication and interaction all took on a new content, often a new depth. The groundwork we had laid often seemed to fall away from under us and we scrambled somewhere else. More had been incorporated, more could be taken for granted, more could be shared. This is a moving ratio and one which never reaches identity, far from it. But there is movement, there is change, there is informing.

Fieldwork, then, is a process of intersubjective construction of liminal modes of communication. Intersubjective means literally more than one subject, but being situated neither quite here nor quite there, the subjects involved do not share a common set of assumptions, experiences, or traditions. Their construction is a public process. Most of this book has focused on these objects which my Moroccan friends and I constructed between us, over time, in order to communicate. That the communication was often painstaking and partial is a central theme. That it was not totally opaque is an equally important theme. It is the dialectic between these poles, ever repeated, never quite the same, which constitutes fieldwork.

Summing up, then, we can say the following.

The first person with whom I had any sustained contact was the Frenchman Maurice Richard. Staying at his hotel was an obligatory first step for Europeans entering into Sefrou (although recently the Moroccan government has opened a luxury hotel). Knowing that his clientele will not be with him long, Richard has developed a persona of cheerful good will, which becomes less and less convincing as he becomes more isolated. The contact with Richard was immediate. There was no language barrier. He was eager to talk. Being an outsider to all of the other Sefrou groups, he had interesting stereotypes of each, which he was more than willing to exchange for a receptive smile. His very accessibility, however, was also revealing of his limitations. He provided entry only to the past, to the last days of colonialism. He was located on the very edge of Sefrou society, its most external point. His corner was easily accessible, but it revealed only the fringes of Moroccan society. Although this subject provided ample material for an inquiry, and was in fact in the process of disappearing forever, my project led me in other directions.

Ibrahim was on the other side of the buffer zone between the French and the Moroccan societies. He had matured during the waning days of the Protectorate and made his career by artfully straddling the line between communities without any confusion as to which side of the line he was on. His speciality was presenting goods and services for external consumption. They were carefully packaged. He was a guide along the main thoroughfares of Sefrou society. His tour was quite helpful for understanding the Ville Nouvelle, but his aid stopped at the walls of the medina. Despite his caution, the first breakthroughs of Otherness occurred with Ibrahim. This professional of the external was, nonetheless, a Moroccan.

My guide through the medina of Sefrou and the transitional zones of Moroccan culture was Ali. My contact with him was the first major step toward a more intimate relationship with Sefrou. He was a floating figure within his own society, living a hand-to-mouth existence in the city. He was a patient, curious, highly imaginative, adventurous, sensuous, and relentlessly perceptive person. My orientation to Moroccan culture as immediacy, as lived experience, came from my friendship with Ali. He had rejected a certain way of life, but not other Moroccan alternatives. He was ascerbic and direct in his criticisms of village ways, but they were insider's jibes.

Ali was also limited by his strengths. Because of his demeanor and antagonism he had almost become an outcast in the village. The insights and orientations which he continued to provide for me throughout the field experience were invaluable. He knowingly and adroitly used the villagers' inhibitions and vulnerabilities against them. Ali was an insider's outsider. His unique vantage point and provocative attitude periodically rescued me from impasses and collective resistance. Ali was, however, now outside village affairs, basically out of touch. He provided little help on the day-to-day level, but could be relied on for vital aid.

So, just as Richard was situated between the two French communities, and Ibrahim between the French and local Moroccan Ville Nouvelle groups, so Ali was situated between the floating population of the medina and his natal village of saint's descendants. All were marginal, all provided help in making transitions from group to group, site to site.

Within Sidi Lahcen itself, the situation became more tightly controlled. The community tacitly (and in some cases explicitly) attempted to situate the anthropologist and thereby control him. The first two young men with whom I worked exemplify this. Mekki, my first informant, literally pushed on me by the villagers, was from Ali's sub-lineage. Not being burdened with family or work obligations, he eagerly sought what to others was a mixed blessing. Unfortunately, he lacked both intelligence and the imaginative ability to objectify his own life-world and then present it to a foreigner. This was an insurmountable handicap. Rashid, my second informant, was everything that Mekki was not; that was his problem. He was imaginative, energetic, curious, intelligent, and was floating, like Ali, except that Rashid's experience was essentially limited to village life. He could have been and was (from time to time) an extremely important informant. But, again like Ali, he aroused strong community disapproval. Rashid's tongue was feared. Everyone, including his father, sought to silence him. Unsure about my presence in the village, they wanted some control over the information I was receiving. Rashid knew a great deal and was eager to convey it. As the Moroccan proverb goes, Those who have no shame, do as they please. And so those with no internal sense of appropriate behavior must be controlled by force. Rashid, unlike Ali, had no power base, no alternative cards to play. In general, he was forced to accede to the community's injunctions, yet he enjoyed violating them whenever the opportunity presented itself.

Malik offered an excellent compromise, both for me and for the community. I had forced my way into Sidi Lahcen, after all, and the villagers feared that ultimately I had come to subvert their religion.

Therefore, it was appropriate that the man who became my central informant was situated on the edge of the most respected of the saintly sub-lineages. This group had a very high rate of endogamous marriage. Malik's father, however, had married a woman not only from outside the sub-lineage but from outside the village. Consequently, as closely attached to this core group as he was emotionally, he was structurally somewhat on its edge, and he overcompensated for it.

He was the perfect representative of orthodoxy. He was proud of his tradition but he had failed to find a traditional role for himself. Impatient with the position of *fqi,* he was stymied in pursuing his own grandiose self-image. A conservative, he lacked institutions to defend. He proved to be the perfect community choice. The elders of his sub-lineage sanctioned his involvement and so did Sergeant Larawi, the most powerful man in the village. They knew they could trust Malik.

Malik, like Ibrahim, was self-controlled, orderly, and reserved. But unlike Ibrahim, he had not made a career of external relations. Malik had remained within the rural world. Malik would have liked to be the internal counterpart of Ibrahim. But no such role existed. He had to improvise as he went along. His "impression management," however, was in constant tension with the inputs of Ali, Rashid, and others. Malik attempted to steer cautiously around sensitive areas. Once challenged, he would yield, but after the early going, he would rarely initiate. As we proceeded, Malik became more dependent on

The fqi takes it easy.

Ben Mohammed:
"a wish for
friendship
may arise quickly
but friendship
does not"

me than I was on him. This helps explain his lack of
sustained resistance on sensitive areas; Ibrahim, no
doubt, would not have backed down so readily.

Many of the political dimensions of the informant
relationship were obviated by Driss ben Mohammed's steadfast adherence to the role of host. This
eventually established the grounds for a dialogue.
Ben Mohammed was internal to the Moroccan tradition. He looked back to his forefather, the
seventeenth-century saint, for guidance in the
modern world. He maintained a belief in the ultimate and unconditional superiority of Islam.

This absolute difference which separated us was
openly acknowledged only at the end of my stay.
We had become friends, we had shown each other
mutual respect and trust. The limits of the situation
were not obscured for either of us. I was for him a
rich member of a dominant civilization about which
he had the profoundest reservations. To me, he was
struggling to revive a cultural universe which I no
longer inhabited and could not ultimately support.
But our friendship tempered our differences. Here
we had come full circle. There were now two subjects facing each other. Each was the product of an
historical tradition which situated and conditioned
him. Each was aware of a profound crisis within that
tradition but still looked back to it for renewal and
solace. We were profoundly Other to each other.

That I would journey to Morocco to confront
Otherness and myself was typical of my culture (or
the parts of it I could accept). That ben Mohammed
would enter into this sort of dialogue without self-
denigration was impressive. My restless and scien-

tifically cloaked wanderings brought me to this mountain village in Morocco. Ben Mohammed sought the wisdom of the reformist saint, yet was willing, even eager, to tell me about him. Through mutual confrontation of our own situations we did establish contact. But this also highlighted our fundamental Otherness. What separated us was fundamentally our past. I could understand ben Mohammed only to the extent that he could understand me—that is to say, partially. He did not live in a crystalline world of immutable Otherness any more than I did. He grew up in an historical situation which provided him with meaningful but only partially satisfactory interpretations of his world, as did I. Our Otherness was not an ineffable essence, but rather the sum of different historical experiences. Different webs of signification separated us, but these webs were now at least partially intertwined. But a dialogue was only possible when we recognized our differences, when we remained critically loyal to the symbols which our traditions had given us. By so doing, we began a process of change.

Selected Bibliography

Theoretical

Berger, Peter, and Thomas Luckmann. *The Social Construction of Reality*. Doubleday, Garden City, New York, 1966.

Duvignaud, Jean. *Le Langage Perdu*. Presses Universitaires de France, Paris, 1973.

Geertz, Clifford. *The Interpretation of Cultures*. Basic Books, New York, 1973.

Ricoeur, Paul. *Le Conflit des Interpretations*. Editions du Seuil, Paris, 1969.

Sartre, Jean-Paul. *Saint Genêt: comédien et martyr*. Gallimard, Paris, 1952.

Schutz, Alfred. *On Phenomenology and Social Relations*. University of Chicago Press, Chicago, 1970.

Anthropological Fieldwork

Beattie, John. *Understanding an African Kingdom: Bunyoro*. Holt, Rinehart and Winston, New York, 1965.

Berreman, Gerald. *Behind Many Masks: Ethnography and Impression Management in a Himalayan Village*. Society for Applied Anthropology, Monograph No. 4, Ithaca, 1962.

Beteille, Andre, and T. N. Madan: *Encounter and Experience: Personal Accounts of Fieldwork*. Vikas Publishing House, Delhi, 1975.

Bowen, Elenore Smith. *Return To Laughter*. Gollanz, London, 1954.